SELLING from TRUST

How to Turn Trust Into a *SALE*

Thomas Morin

HERE I AM
PUBLISHING, LLC

Copyright © 2026 Thomas Morin

All rights reserved. No part of this book may be reproduced in any form or by any electronic or mechanical means, including information storage and retrieval systems, without permission in writing from the publisher, except by reviewers, who may quote brief passages in a review.

ISBN 978-1-958032-40-4
Printed in the United States of America.
Registered in the Library of Congress.

Designed by Molly Beck, Graphic Artist

Published by Here I Am Publishing, LLC.
info@hereiampublishingllc.com
Sandi Huddleston-Edwards, Publisher
780 Monterrosa Drive
Myrtle Beach, SC 29572

About this Book

Salespeople today often live in an environment full of force-fed, top-down selling systems, where they are trained and directed to repeat the same monotonic, robotic words with every customer, regardless of how their customer prefers to be spoken to. In *Selling from Trust*, Thomas Morin offers a more human-centered approach that's based on the art of the sale, rather than the science. It's not a selling strategy, but a communication strategy that's built around how customers prefer to communicate when they're developing their own personal relationships.

Thomas's approach focuses on the core human values and experiences that stimulate relationships to grow through honesty, respect, actively listening to each other, and, most importantly, trust. Each of these basic human components helps calm the anxious customer's fears and opens his/her mind to be more receptive to and purchase from a salesperson he/she might have been initially intimidated by.

In its basic form, *Selling from Trust* is a how-to, bottom-up approach to winning the customer first, and only then transitioning to a product presentation with a customer who is more willing to listen and consider what a salesperson has to say, instead of running away from the typical sales pitch heard from one salesperson to the next. It's a winning approach that can be repeated with every customer because it's about the customer rather than the selling system.

The sales process is a process that, through repetition and finesse over time, gets stronger, more precise, and can lead to more profitable deals and help to establish a solid path to referrals with new customers going forward.

What people who bought *Selling From Trust* have to say!

"Selling from Trust offers valuable lessons and actionable ideas for anyone in a client-facing role. Whether you're a new trainee or a seasoned veteran, there's something in it for everyone. Readers are shown that at its core, selling is about listening to another person's wants and needs and helping him/her achieve desired goals. Lessons in human interaction and relationship building are timeless, so you'll likely find yourself coming back to certain chapters to get back to the basics and reinforce good habits long after your first read." — Ryan Meca, Vice President, Merrill Lynch

"This book gets at the heart of what sales is really about—people and mastering the connection between the salesperson and the customer. It shows us how to replace anxiety with calmness, concern with trust, and rejection with confidence. Each chapter feels like a roadmap for professional growth and achieving results in selling." — Diane Luksis, Metabolic Health Coach

"Trust is at the heart of every sale, from the very first impression to whether the customer ever comes back. This book demonstrates how salespeople can establish trust from the outset, while also guiding customers through the challenging aspects of the job, such as customer anxiety and rejection. With down-to-earth strategies and real stories, it lays out a clear path on how to turn trust into long-term sales success." — Erik Betz, Training & Development Specialist

"Thomas's book has shown me the best approach and how best to listen to my customers to prove that I have their best interests in mind and to help build the comfort and trust I need to close the sale. His book has also helped me manage customer rejection and slow sales periods, as well as overcome some of the stresses associated with commission-based sales." — Charles Weitz, Roofing Contractor Salesperson

"Selling from Trust offers practical insights into better understanding my customers and how to build solid trust that can lead to referrals. Thomas's advice is grounded in success and real experience, providing thoughtful strategies all salespeople can use to improve customer skills and hone their craft. It was a great refresher for me!" — Adam Isabella, Insurance Broker

Dedication

As I thought about what motivated me to write this, my third book on helping salespeople be better, more successful, and, of course, make more money, I remembered the one thing that inspired me more than anything else to be the best salesperson I could be…and it was the customer. Specifically, it was the customers who, after spending two, three, or four hours listening to my product demonstrations, said *"No"* to buying from me.

Salespeople everywhere constantly battle with how to handle the stream of rejection they face in selling because it is very, very frustrating. Few of us are built to feel pleasure in anyone consistently saying *"No"* to us in business or life. I see so many potentially great salespeople join their company with great goals, dreams, and intentions but give up and leave after a year or two, right about the time they were starting to figure it out and start to see the fruits of their labor in real money.

With that in mind, I am dedicating *Selling from Trust* to all the customers who said that they didn't want to buy from me, despite my best efforts and hard work. Why? Because it was this group that drove me to look in the mirror and realize that I was the problem and needed to make changes, not them.

I needed to understand that I couldn't paint with a broad brush of my company's selling system, talking to and treating each customer in the same way, when each was actually a different personality. The "one size fits all" approach just didn't work, and it forced me to remember that customers are people, just like me. I realized that my way of communicating worked great with some customers but not so much with others.

So, I started to approach each customer interaction from square one, listening more than talking to learn about him/her before I started telling the customer about me or my product. I realized that to talk turkey with him/her, I had to realize what kind of turkey the customer was, how he/she spoke and wanted to be spoken to, and how I could adjust to HIM/HER rather than making the customer adjust to me. I never abandoned our selling system, and, in fact, it became more effective. It was just that I had to build comfort, rapport, and trust before unleashing it on him/her, and that led me to the real meaning of selling.

I also started to think about how I grew personal relationships, how to help others trust me, and how much better we both felt from that. I realized that the establishment of trust was the conduit for almost everything else that was to come in person and in business, which made me passionate about that as a priority. As a salesperson, I used to go home and say to my wife, "If I can get them to trust me, I can sell them the state of Alaska." As we advanced, especially in any business-related conversation, I made the establishment of trust a priority, whether I was the salesperson or the customer…and it worked like a charm.

For all the customers who said *"No"* over the years, *thank you*. I owe you and dedicate this book to you because it forced me to get better, to be better, or lose the opportunity sales has given to me.

Introduction

As I continue on my passionate journey to help salespeople on the road to continuous improvement, increasing sales, earning more money, and erasing some of the long- standing negative stereotypes, I am constantly challenging myself on the best approach I can take to help guide them to make better decisions about how they can impact their performance, results, and perceptions.

The first thing to realize is just how many people in our lives fall under the umbrella of selling. If you stop and think about how many people provide goods or services to us that we individually need to accept or reject them and their services, you'll realize that there are many more than we might think. We rely heavily on doctors, dentists, financial managers, investment advisors, pastors, and numerous other professionals, making decisions based on our trust in them personally, as well as their level of competence. This opens the spectrum to illustrate the value of trust-based buying and selling with all of us.

In trying to earn trust, many companies across various industries fail to provide sufficient training for their salespeople on the steps needed to effectively connect with nervous or anxious customers by using an approach that can help them relax and enjoy the shopping (and hopefully buying) experience.

In too many cases, companies tend to hire extreme extroverts for their sales staff, thinking their sparkling personalities and abilities to communicate alone would be enough to build rapport and get through any nervousness caused by bad experiences the customers had with the salespeople down the street. WRONG. Why? Because they talk too much.

I am not saying businesses should start hiring only introverts, but they need to search for *hybrid* individuals who can move between listening and speaking, as the situation requires. They need to find, interview, and hire individuals who have the personalities to be outgoing and vibrant when the situation calls for it but also have the discretion to be quiet and listen when the customer needs to be heard.

I have witnessed times when competent but introverted candidates interested in applying for a sales position shy away from it because they feel they can't be outgoing enough to be hired. That's a mistake, as I have seen many introverted people be successful in sales. Still, they must be comfortable being uncomfortable when a situation requires them to take the lead in a sales process or initiate a conversation with a customer to help him/her relieve anxiety.

I have also seen many extroverts achieve high success in sales, but their inability to pull back and listen when the situation calls for it often results in no sale. It's especially evident in the early stages of a "meet & greet," when a nervous customer deserves every opportunity to feel comfortable speaking, but the talkative salesperson, trying to prove his/her worth, overcomes the customer.

Customers today are different from those of years ago. They appear to be more stressed out and sensitive than in past years. They are confused by misinformation, conflicted by differing opinions on COVID vaccines, and are nervous about higher interest rates, combined with a rise in the cost of living. Finally, they are faced with the increasing need for people to take stronger political sides and defend them with energy and vigor. All of this has contributed to putting an already anxious customer seemingly more on edge.

In addition, customers are much more educated when they walk into a business to make a large purchase, having spent a great deal of time researching the product they are interested in looking at. Today, they typically do much more research on reviews and comments of previous customers online as well to get a read on how a company does business and if it is reputable and honest. As a result, customers tend to walk in having a much better idea of what they want to look at and why, which puts pressure on salespeople to be better listeners than in previous years. Customers no longer start from *square one*, as they have in the past.

There are also times when customers fall in love with the wrong thing online before even entering a business, which puts even more pressure on a salesperson to talk them out of making a bad decision, and the salesperson typically faces some opposition in doing so.

All the above have made shopping and buying a more emotional exercise than in the past, when logical thinking was the typical customer approach, which puts more pressure on salespeople to be more people-minded and less sales-minded.

A few other things have become clear to me as I train and coach salespeople across the country. One was that the top 20% really do excel in the techniques and skills needed to help their anxious customer relax for as long as it takes before even considering putting him/her in front of the product. As a result, this group had a much better chance of helping their customers feel a sense of comfort, which helps to build rapport and form the foundation of trust needed to feel comfortable buying two, three, or four hours later.

All too often, the bottom 25% (non-performing group) frankly made no effort to do any of this, typically hurried their customers in front of their products, and wasted hours showing it without realizing they never gave their customers a chance to like and trust them. That was almost always the customer who walked out, saying, "I want to go home and think about it," never to be heard from again. It was and is my view that this group needs to either change their approach or consider leaving the sales business and seek an opportunity in another non-sales-related workplace.

Through all this, there are another 55% or so who have emerged as beacons of hope. This group works very hard to model the top 20%, being successful at times but just not consistently so. However, their commitment, effort, and motivation to constantly improve IS there, and THIS group is who this book is written for. Most in this group have the potential to improve and, with time, effort, and use of every minute of downtime to get better can make the jump up to the top 20% and stay there.

Selling from the Bottom Up is a continuation of the critical step I wrote about in my last book, *No Trust, No Sale* where salespeople learned how to overcome obstacles salespeople typically face in their journey to build trust with their customers. In that book, we reviewed how they can establish a foundation of trust with customers and then use that as a basis for working with them in a way that helps them feel that shopping and buying are on their terms. Customers must be allowed to be comfortable to alleviate the anxiety with which they walk in the front door and to feel listened to, one of the biggest complaints they frequently have about salespeople. To lay the groundwork for this, salespeople must have the ability to connect with customers in a manner the customer prefers, not the salespeople.

If not, this will create an environment where customers feel the salesperson is focusing more on the buying than the shopping, which typically stresses customers out.

It's true a salesperson can occasionally get lucky and sell something without establishing comfort and trust with his/her customers. There are also times when price is the ONLY consideration with a customer and yet other times the customer falls completely in love with a product and buys it at any price. However, if those times happened more than just a rare exception, more salespeople would have much more lucrative careers than they do.

Selling from Trust is the transition that helps salespeople leverage the solid trust they have built with their customers through the other key steps they need to take to complete the sale and ultimately have the customers say "Yes" to buying from them.

Trust-based selling isn't a *one-trick pony*. It's a core principle designed to build a long- lasting, personal relationship with your customer, allowing for not only an enjoyable sales process but also the continuation of repeat sales over many years. It's designed to be similar to two friends who trust each other and don't hold back thoughts and emotions, even in a sales process. It's this kind of customer relationship that becomes personal, and friendships emerge from it.

One main benefit from this, other than the obvious, is referrals. No sales career can be successful in the long term without building it around a referral business. Referral sales tend to be the most profitable because they start with a recommendation from a trusted friend to another, which removes much of the underlying anxiety and tension that typically occurs between a salesperson and a customer, at least in the early stages.

When customers go through encounters with salespeople they truly enjoyed, they can't wait to tell their friends and family about it, which motivates referral customers to consider buying even if they hadn't previously considered it. Think of a neighbor who buys a new RV, and loves his/her salesperson, which leads to a growing love for traveling and camping and then shares their wonderful experiences with other neighbors. Pretty soon everyone on the street has a camper, they're planning annual group camping trips, and the triangle rises upward and gets wider. This is word of mouth marketing at its best.

I have seen this so many times in the neighborhoods I have lived in. A neighbor puts in a pool or puts up a fence around his/her property, and eventually, everyone has one. Regardless of the reason, these things tend to build on each other, and that benefits the salesperson, as long as his/her process is built around the customer and not him/her.

To help get things started, Chapter 1 kicks things off with a review of the cat-and-mouse game played every day between customers and salespeople. Unfortunately, too many salespeople are obsessed with taking control over their customers, as well as the selling process, and have developed a horrible reputation. This becomes the FIRST obstacle they must overcome to gain the customers' trust…yet, very few of them accept this and, as a result, blow right past it to hurry customers out in front of their products, living under the false perception that doing so will overcome all the emotional issues their customers might have with them.

This book is also designed to help salespeople realize they can win at this game, only if they realize that the customer is in the driver's seat because they're the ones with the credit card. I hope that following the guidelines in this book will greatly help salespeople change their thinking and, ultimately, get out of their own way.

To the salespeople reading this, work with me here…if you listen, I can help you understand that you can achieve and maintain control through trust, while at the same time allow the customer to feel like he/she has it. Why? Because trust and control are subconscious requirements for him/her. Building and sustaining trust is completely achievable for any salesperson if he/she is open-minded. The salesperson needs to set aside preconceived thoughts of sell, sell, sell to accept the benefits and invest the time to build the sales process with trust if he/she follows through with the steps outlined in this book.

If you think about it, it's no different than any other personal relationship that we build. We want our relationships to stand the test of time, and they have a better chance if they're built with trust. Salesperson/Customer relationships are built the same way, maybe even more so because they involve the exchange of hard-earned money.

So, take the journey through this book, and let's work together to help build the successful sales career you envisioned and the commissions that go with it when you decide to jump into this great sales career opportunity.

Best of luck to you!

Contents

1. The Chess Game with Customers 1
2. The Anxiety Factor 15
3. Adjusting to Your Customer's Type 27
4. Building A Foundation of Trust 37
5. Product Selling or Relationship Selling? 49
6. The "Three Minutes of Discomfort" 55
7. Situational Salesmanship 63
8. *Collaborative* Demonstrations 79
9. Preparing for Objections 87
10. Closing the Sale 97
11. *Legendary* Follow-Through 105
12. Overcoming Obstacles 115
13. Referrals Based on Trust 127
14. Managing Self-Development 133
15. "I Want to Go Home and Think About It" 143
16. A Call to Action 157
Appendix ....

1

The Chess Game with Customers

The human connection between a customer and a salesperson is an interesting phenomenon to observe, especially during the first few minutes of meeting each other. What's interesting is that if you look closely at their facial expressions and body language, most of us will be able to draw fairly accurate conclusions about how things are going, even if we can't hear a word each is saying. Most of us have at least a basic understanding of what normal human behavior is when observing two people talking to each other. Why? Because our non-verbal cues and body language tend to give us a fairly accurate perception of how we are each feeling.

If it's *this easy to figure out*, then why do so many salespeople struggle in the early stages of meeting a customer for the first time? If you look closely, it seems so uncomfortable and awkward for many of them. In many cases, it seems obvious that both the salesperson and the customer get so distracted by their preconceived assumptions, life experiences, and often inaccurate perceptions of each other that it takes their focus away from how to co-exist together.

Customers tend to worry about whether the salespeople will be honest with them, and the salespeople want to prove their knowledge and competence to the customers to increase the chance that the customers will buy something. Salespeople often anticipate that customers can be anxious, edgy, and sometimes angry about having to work with them, and as a result, sometimes they work too hard to overcome a problem before one exists.

Both the customer and salesperson also have specific objectives that can be highly uncomfortable, raising the tension and anxiety for both. This changes the game entirely. The often desperate, commission-based salesperson, who struggles to sell only 30% of the customers he/she works with, has a sales system he/she are directed to follow, along with a sales manager who is nagging him/her about performance and results. Then you have a customer, who typically wants a great product at a great price and has an electric fence around his/her credit card, caused by high interest rates and other bills to pay in a down economy. Both have a great deal at stake with each new interaction that tends to make them both nervous and edgy.

When you add in the normal stresses of life we face to this scenario, we're left with a confusing, stressful situation that's like an emotional chess game. In the typical interaction between a salesperson and a customer, there sometimes ends up being a winner and a loser and as a result, no sale. What starts as a potentially enjoyable time toward a win-win conclusion often ends up with one or both parties quite cranky about wasting two, three, or four hours, often without achieving their desired result.

The sad part about all this is that it *could* be just two people helping each other toward a common goal *if* they would just let it happen. There is an opportunity right in front of them to enjoy the mutual benefits and value in a salesperson/customer interaction, yet often they are not successful, as they each have different goals, concerns, and are unwilling to meet in the middle. They both want to win. The salesperson wants a full gross deal, and the customer wants something awesome for almost nothing.

Customers buy cars, furniture, homes, and other things, and in most cases must end up working with a salesperson, and frankly, they do not like that. What contributes to this problem is that some current salespeople frankly should be in another line of work because the job just doesn't fit them. However, many are attracted to the lucrative earning potential, and let's face it, we all need a job.

On top of all this, if you shop long enough, most of us will have a bad experience with a salesperson at some point in our lives. When we do, we tend not to forget it, so it's typical that the next few times we work with one, we bring that bad memory through the front door with us. This often leads to incorrect assumptions that the next experience will be just as bad and maybe worse. This causes many customers to initially greet salespeople with anxiety, apprehension, and nervousness, making the interaction much more challenging than it needs to be.

When customers walk in with memories of bad prior salesperson encounters and have anxiety because of it, there's a great deal of work that has to be done to undo that before salespeople can get to step one. All too often, salespeople overlook this. Too many companies tend to hire extroverted salespeople who talk too much. In their efforts to sound knowledgeable, some salespeople come off as phony or arrogant, which makes overcoming these negative perceptions in those first few moments much more difficult than it needs to be. This causes a blockade in getting to know each other and is one of the reasons why 70% of customers walk out without buying anything, regardless of what they're looking to buy.

One way to prove this point is to observe customers walking through the front door of any business that employs salespeople and their initial actions. The nervous, anxious customer will come in the front door and often take significant measures to avoid being approached by a salesperson. Some will use evasive tactics, such as asking where the restroom is and then taking an alternate route to the area where the product or merchandise is located to view it without a salesperson's involvement. What's more interesting is that this happens even when a customer is *fully aware* he/she will need a salesperson's help to find the perfect product. Many customers walk in with specific, non-negotiable objectives, regardless of what they are shopping for, resulting in an emotional *chess game* with the salesperson.

Now that we have established this, what can we do about it?

A good starting point for salespeople is to be keenly aware of this potential for customer anxiety and to be conscious of the clues that might reveal it. Most salespeople are aware that some of their competitors may be unqualified or unprofessional, which can leave emotional scars on their next customer. They also need to understand that many of their customers (if not most) have their own set of objectives regarding how they want to play the salesperson game. Those bad previous salesperson experiences cause customers to adjust their approach and expectations when working with the next one. As you might expect, this makes the job of the next salesperson they see a great deal more difficult. Some of the demands customers end up having with salespeople are as follows.

Be Honest & Trustworthy
Very simply, customers expect 100% honesty 100% of the time. Period. This is a non-negotiable expectation for all customers. All a salesperson has to do is be dishonest ONE time, and he/she is done. There will be no sale today, and when the customer leaves, he/she will tell everyone about it.

Be Willing to Listen to Them
Companies that hire extroverts run the risk of having a salesperson who (to use an industry term) *shows up and throws up* (verbally) all over the customer, which is highly offensive to him/her. Not being listened to is one of the biggest issues customers have with salespeople. Hiring introverts doesn't solve the problem either because they tend to be too quiet, often intimidate the customer, or act strangely. What is needed is someone who can move back and forth between being an introvert and an extrovert based on the customer's needs, as the situation dictates. Successful salespeople today must have chameleon-like tendencies, being

able to adjust their style, *especially* in the early stages of the "meet & greet." Mostly, though, it's to listen more than talk because this is the time when the customer has information you need in order to put him/her in front of the product that makes sense. Salespeople don't need to change their personalities to do this; they just need to be better listeners and be more aware of what the customers are saying about what they want and why they want it.

Select the Right Product for Them
Customers expect the salesperson (or sales manager) to select ONLY products that make sense for them and NOT what the sales manager wants to move out of inventory or has the best commission for the salesperson. This happens more than it should, as businesses have a high need to move out old inventory and to sell higher-profit products.

Have Strong Product Knowledge
Customers not only expect salespeople to *know their stuff* when it comes to the product they sell, but they expect them to *master it*. They also expect them to explain (in detail) how each option or feature *can benefit them or solve a problem for them*. Customers also tend to compare one salesperson against the next in this key area and want to work with the most competent one available. If the salesperson down the street does a better job with this, the customer will go somewhere else to work with him/her.

Move at the Customer's Pace
It's frustrating to me that some companies place time limits on how quickly they expect the initial interview to take before getting their customers in front of their products. This is a grave mistake, as some customers just need more time to get comfortable than others. I will discuss this in detail in later chapters, but salespeople must uncover the pace their customers want to move at and adjust their presentation to that. Rushing them because another customer is coming in at 3:00 p.m. will kill any chance of the customer achieving a feeling of comfort with them. Reschedule the next appointment before you even get started, or you will lose *both* deals.

If You Don't Know the Answer, DON'T MAKE UP ONE
This is a major flaw with salespeople and is a red flag for their customers.

Of course, they all want to sound smart to gain credibility with the customer, but most customers can quickly see right through a made-up answer. More customers than ever are researching products online before going to a business, and as a result, they are a great deal more informed about them than just five years ago. Making up answers is deceptive, and lying is a deal-breaker. If you do this even once, you are done with this customer—and by the way, they will also tell fifty friends about this incident and ruin the chance of many more customers coming into the business. It's a one-and-done scenario.

Focus More on the Shopping Than Getting the Sale
Customers know that a commission salesperson will be trying hard to sell them something, which creates extra pressure and anxiety for them. They prefer that salespeople stop viewing this as a win-lose situation because much of the time, even when they say "No," it doesn't always mean they're not buying. Often, the word "*No*" actually means *not right now*, and they may very well be back to buy from them tomorrow or in the near future if the salesperson handles that with grace and professionalism. Constantly trying to close them throughout the sales process is a major turnoff for customers as they often want to enjoy shopping and buying at their own pace.

How Salespeople Pressure Customers
All too often, salespeople go out of their way to try to *trap* customers into buying by saying something like, "If you don't buy it today, it won't be here tomorrow." Customers often perceive that it's one person trying to outsmart them, and they do not like this. Sometimes this perception is caused by conflicting personalities or styles, but often it's a result of a salesperson trying to put a square peg into a round hole. Customers almost always want to be sold in a way THEY feel comfortable, not necessarily the way the company's standard selling system dictates.

Company Selling Systems

Some companies pay a great deal of money for a *selling system* from an outside company or vendor. Training on these systems tends to be more consistent than for companies that don't use one because representatives from the outside vendor typically provide it. The downside to these systems is that every customer is taken through the sales process in the same way with the same words, phrases, rapport builders, and closing lines and is not treated as an individual.

Many customers overhear other salespeople saying the same things, eventually sensing the robotic nature in how salespeople say words or phrases, which just doesn't sound natural. They often sound robotic or rehearsed, which makes most customers very suspicious and defensive. It's a system that may make sense based on psychological science but often isn't practical. All too often, because most salespeople don't commit to it enough to master it, it comes off sounding choppy and impersonal. Customers want to feel special, and they don't feel that way when hearing a salesperson use the same words as with the customer twenty feet away.

Knowledge and Competence

Most salespeople want to be perceived by their customers as having strong knowledge about both their products and the selling process, and many do work very hard at that. However, far too many companies have training programs that leave most of the responsibility of learning the technical aspects of their product (and its features) completely up to each salesperson. Individual motivation varies from one to the next, so inconsistency is quite possible between salespeople. This is especially true with the new salesperson, but some experienced ones are just not as motivated as they should be.

Unmotivated salespeople can quickly burn through a high number of customers without a sale before sales managers realizes they aren't working hard enough independently to have even basic product knowledge. Either way, if a customer senses the salesperson doesn't know what he/she is talking about, the salesperson will be creative in making up excuses as to why the customer will have to leave the premises.

This might sound like unreal expectations by customers, but they're the ones with the credit card, and they demand and expect a great deal from salespeople.

Salespeople are expected to follow company procedures, ownership preferences, and sometimes proven philosophical approaches. Everything most salespeople do is designed to result in one thing: having the customer purchase before leaving, whether the sales process is business-to-customer or business-to-business. Almost all have a product and/or service to sell and have a process to make that happen with success or failure based largely on the salesperson's execution. It's a simple conclusion: you either sold it or you didn't, and failure is not an option.

Here are some of the major things that typically end up on a salesperson's chessboard.

Know Your Product (or Service)
This is simple and to the point; you must know what you're selling, inside and out. Most companies do a fairly decent job of training staff on at least enough product information to be able to demonstrate important features and information to their customers. However, despite the critical nature of this, some companies fall well below expectations on programs or systems needed to improve the competence of their sales staff. Overall, though, most give a good-faith effort in this area even if they fall short.

Control the Sales Process
Many businesses have a sales process or use a *selling system*. Some are more extensive than others. Salespeople typically work hard to move customers through the shopping (and hopefully buying) process while trying to find products the customers like within their budget. They also develop shopping systems that can lead to a purchase. Some customers love window shopping, which gets them off track, confused,

and overwhelmed by looking at too many products in one visit. As a result, it's easy for them to feel rushed by the salesperson and end up leaving without purchasing anything, so it's critical for the salesperson to keep them on track.

Handle Objections
Companies (and salespeople) spend a great deal of time thinking about and projecting what customers' objections might be, so they are ready to respond to them. They tend to practice canned responses, hoping that will get the customer over the hump and onto buying. This is one area where salespeople can do better, and we will review this in detail in a later chapter.

Communicate Company Philosophy
Most companies have a few core systems and philosophies they use to build customer loyalty and do an admirable job of getting that message out to their customers. Some examples are military discounts, competitive in-house financing, great product warranties, the best service after the sale, and so on. Overall, most do a solid job of teaching programs, advertising them, and delivering them.

Bringing in a Closer
After the salesperson brings the customer as far as the salesperson can to get the customer to buy, some companies bring in a *closer*, which could be a sales manager or designated person to come in, offer a few extra freebies, and generally put another level of pressure on the customer to buy. This often starts with handing out a few free things to entice a customer to say yes, and if that doesn't work, then the hammer comes out for the hard close until the customer does say "Yes." Frankly, customers hate this because it's too high pressure for them.

The question is where on the chessboard do the objectives between customers and salespeople begin to mesh with each other? Here are a few things that salespeople need to do differently, and your customers will feel more like they won, whether they've agreed to say yes to buying or not.

Build TRUST
We will spend a great deal of time talking about building trust throughout this book and especially in Chapter 3. Price is always important, and the product or service is important too, but your customer WILL NOT say yes to buying today if he/she doesn't feel that he/she can trust you. People buy from people they like and trust, and that hasn't changed in 150 years. It doesn't matter what the economy is, what interest rates are, or what product is available. Customers MUST feel trust in their salespeople.

Focus on the SHOPPING More Than the BUYING
Spending more time helping the customers enjoy the shopping process is very important to them, and it will be easier to convince them if they are being led through each step to buy the perfect products (that's in their budgets) by a knowledgeable, trusted partner who has their best interests in mind, rather than being forced to buy the products by a pushy salesperson.

Respect the Customer's Budget
Once you establish the customer's budget, do not show him/her a product or service that's above it. In fact, refuse to do so, at least initially. Showing respect for the stated budget will prove to the customer that you're not a salesperson who is trying to *upsell* him/her, another big fear. When showing a product, begin with the least expensive product that easily fits the budget. If you have built trust, when he/she sees how many features are lacking in this lowest-priced product, the customer will likely be more open to expanding his/her budget number on his/her own. Part of showing this respect is allowing THE CUSTOMER to control this decision, rather than trying to *upsell*.

Pre-Empt Customer Objections
Most objections arise from a poor presentation: a salesperson not having product knowledge or customer discomfort caused by a lack of trust. Mastering product, combined with a complete understanding of the problem the customer needs to solve (or a need he/she must fill)

will reduce most objections not associated with price. A customer who doesn't trust his/her salesperson will also manufacture false objections as an excuse not to buy because he/she just isn't comfortable with the salesperson and will do so even when not knowing why.

No Hard Close
If you need to hard-close a customer, you have not done the things listed above. Once you build trust, focus more on the shopping than the selling, are respectful of the customer's budget, and do a world-class product presentation that solves a problem (or a need) for him/her, your deal should be 98% closed. If the close is a battle, it's not the CUSTOMER; it's YOU.

To prevent this from happening with the next customers after the current customer leaves, salespeople must take the time to replay the entire visit in their minds. They should do a step-by-step review to assess where they might have missed a step, so it's not repeated with the next customer.

After all this, there are a few additional ways salespeople and customers can meet the customer in the middle. Believe it or not, a great way for a salesperson to build credibility with a customer is to say, "I don't know."

WHAT! Yes, It's true!

If you don't know the answer to a question, it's best to *say that you don't know* but that you'll pull in the resources around you to find the answer immediately. So many salespeople are unwilling to do this. In my early days, when I was learning the job, there were many times when I really didn't know the answer to a question. I immediately got a sales manager, factory representative, another salesperson, or someone else on the phone who had the answer. I would say to the customer, "Let me make a quick call to get your question answered, and then we'll BOTH know the answer." After doing so two, three, or even four times in a customer visit, the customer will actually start to perceive you as the answer man/woman and that you will not lie or make up an answer to his/her question. That's an honest approach and builds trust and credibility with your customer.

Another way to meet in the middle is to adjust your selling style to the customer. I reviewed this in my last book called *No Trust, No Sale*. If your customer is a quiet, detailed, analytical type, you shouldn't answer questions with general answers. This particular style of customer wants a specific, detailed answer, backed up with written documentation and facts if it is possible. Yet, the expressive, good-time customer wants to enjoy the shopping process and have some fun for two to four hours and not get bogged down in paperwork and details. You need to assess who is standing in front of you and adjust your presentation to that customer.

Lastly, if you're not sure how to best serve your customer in a way that is expected, ASK! If you have a customer who isn't verbal about what he/she expects and doesn't exhibit non-verbal cues to help you figure that out, then ask the customer. Simply asking the customer, "To give you the best possible service today, what can I do to help you feel comfortable, relaxed, and enjoy our shopping time together?" It's that simple. Unless the customer is extremely introverted, most customers will tell you exactly what they want and expect.

There will be a few that won't. Why? Because they're too uncomfortable and anxious to be honest in answering that question. So, let's take a close look at why that happens in Chapter 2. We'll look at some real-life scenarios, what causes them, and what you can do about them.

2

The Anxiety Factor

Before you can truly turn trust into sales success, you need to have at least some understanding of the role that anxiety plays in your customers' thoughts, fears, mindsets, and perceptions as they walk into a business and realize they will be working with a salesperson.

We live in an increasingly anxious world today in numerous areas of our lives. Things seem to be coming at us from all directions, don't they? All this has a carry-over effect on many other parts of daily living. When you combine this with the stress customers tend to feel when spending money, along with the strong need for salespeople to sell something to earn a living, the emotions involved surely become a factor in the whole process.

To enjoy success in selling, salespeople must first understand and accept that customer anxiety is a real issue that plays a significant role in both the shopping and buying processes. (Sadly, some salespeople perceive this as a weakness and use that as an opportunity to take advantage of the customer.)

On the surface, it's typical to think that making a large purchase would be done logically because of the amount of money involved, and much of the time, it is. A buyer creates a systematic thought of what is needed and why, what problem has to be solved, what money is available to spend, and what products and features are considered to meet those needs. It all makes sense, right?

Not so fast…taking customers' hard-earned money out of their wallets can be a highly emotional event, as well, and the dynamics of the process can change entirely when there's another person (a salesperson) involved to help them do this. Why? Because now you not only have the customer, a product, and its features. You have the added consideration of an alternative personality you're not sure you trust involved with it. Sometimes, this works out well, but too often, it doesn't.

When customers work with a salesperson they have met just moments before, they aren't yet sure if the salesperson knows the product, whether his/her intentions are sincere, and most importantly, if he/she is honest or not. This typically creates a great deal of stress for the customer.

It's natural for the anxious customers to guard their words and emotions and be very withdrawn with salespeople, especially in the early stages. They tend to proceed cautiously and often guard (and sometimes withhold) important information the salespeople need until they're comfortable. This is even a bigger problem when shopping for a car or RV, which are high-ticket items with potentially dozens to look at. Most customers, especially those who are anxious, tend to quickly tire and lose interest after demonstrations on just three or four products that don't end up being a good fit for them because it's physically and emotionally exhausting. Salespeople need to recognize and address this anxiety in the first few minutes to help customers feel comfortable before attempting to get any honest answers on what they want and how much they're willing to pay for it.

Although this is a fairly normal situation for any customer buying with the help of a salesperson, if those personalities are cluttered with inaccurate misconceptions about each other, the whole thing can become more complicated than it needs to be. Two people in the same situation can easily misinterpret what has been said or done, which can contribute to misreading each other. Misconceptions about each other can be formed before a salesperson and customer even meet, based on previous experience with others. This can make a fairly simple process a great deal more difficult, and it happens daily in the sales business. Sounds like a whole lot of emotional baggage, doesn't it?

So, what's the cause of this anxiety?

Although the customer is the main player in this process, for now, let's start with the salesperson. Most customers don't realize that salespeople have their own anxiety to deal with, which is a typical part of a sales job, even before they walk in the front door.

To start with in a commission business, if you don't sell, you aren't getting paid, at least for many months of the year. Most sales businesses have peak seasons and off seasons. During the slowest months of the year, salespeople typically must handle a constant barrage of accountability from their sales managers, then go home with no paycheck (because business was slow). Then they try to explain to their spouses why there is no money to pay the bills. I promise you, that's real anxiety, and those are real emotions.

If a salesperson isn't selling, then the business is not only not making money, but they're also burning through customers that another salesperson might have sold something to. Selling is a "what have you done for me lately" business, so the risk of being let go always hangs over the salespersons' heads because they're not meeting their goals. That's real anxiety and real emotions.

To survive this, salespeople must possess a high level of confidence to handle 70% or more of their customers saying "*No*" to buying, without taking it personally or having it affect them emotionally. It sounds easy, but it's not. This is especially true when a shopping process seems to be going great, but then the customer chooses not to buy anything.

Salespeople need a mental toughness that might have to be acquired or learned over time, since some don't have it when they are hired. Being a salesperson requires a grit that many tend to underestimate when they start working in the sales field because the job brings with it some heavy emotional challenges. If you think about our daily lives, *none of us* wants to hear a constant barrage of "*Nos*" regardless of what the subject matter is and whether it's at home or work; yet, in sales, it's commonplace. That's real anxiety and real emotions.

There are also situations where customers fall in love with the wrong thing for whatever reason. There could be a sale sitting right in front of a salesperson, who then has to find the courage to advise the customer not to buy because the product isn't right for him/her. It's the right thing to do, but in doing so, you will lose a sale in the process. Then the salesperson has to deal with the internal battle: the need to make money and his/her integrity, over whether to make some cash or do the right thing, again real anxiety and real emotions.

When you think about customers and the emotions they deal with when making major buying decisions, it's even less enjoyable for them. I feel like most of us, at one point or another, have worked with a salesperson who was not knowledgeable, not competent, dishonest, too pushy, or frankly, just a jerk to deal with. Customers are known for having long memories with bad salespeople experiences, and this situation typically leaves a pretty deep scar on most of them. Human nature being what it is, it often causes customers to *paint with a broad brush* and put ALL salespeople in the same box, even when the next one they work with doesn't deserve it.

This situation can be an issue in any industry that sells products or services, whether to customers or other businesses. Here is what some of my contributors have to say.

Diane Luksis, a metabolic health coach from Atlanta, Georgia, says that her experience in dealing with customers is that "most customers think that salespeople can be too pushy and tend to feel pressured into buying something, rather than being guided into buying what they want."

Adam Isabella, an insurance broker from upstate New York, says, "I also think that some customers don't fully understand what to expect when they walk into a dealership or business and what it takes to complete that transaction."

Brian Osborn, a real estate agent, says, "If I find that my client is nervous in a transaction, I need to help him/her talk and get everything out, by being a great listener and helping them answer any questions or concerns they might have."

When you talk about the emotional effect in buying, nothing can be more intimidating than investing hundreds of thousands or in some cases, millions of dollars, with an investment firm.

Ryan Meca, a vice president and financial advisor at Merrill Lynch, says, "When a client previously worked with a salesperson who was pushy or aggressive, that uncomfortable feeling is tough to shake off, and that puts the customer on edge, especially in the early stages of a sales setting."

The emotional scars left by these negative experiences can leave an imprint in customers' minds, with a great deal of unfair apprehension and negative perceptions of salespeople. Even if a bad experience happens only once, it's often easy for them to forget that most salespeople have every intention of providing a great experience to help them purchase something that best fits their needs and budget.

As a result, some customers can respond with a highly aggressive approach of walking into a business and going on offense by embarrassing, bullying, or treating a salesperson disrespectfully. As bad as this sounds, some customers enjoy this and do it just for the sport of it. It's retaliation for them, and they know that most of the time, they can get away with it because *they're the customer* and the "customer is always right." Some do it because they think it strengthens their negotiating position or leverage to make a deal. Ugh.

Although most companies would back a salesperson who is being screamed at or bullied by a customer, some don't allow the salesperson to push back under *any circumstances*. Of course, as they say, "Two wrongs don't make a right," but that's real anxiety and real emotions for salespeople, who need to be prepared to handle this type of customer at any given moment.

Simply put, being in sales isn't for the faint of heart. It's often a test of confidence, will, courage, and mental toughness all thrown into one, but it's necessary for long-term survival in a sales environment. The good news is that over time, through learning from failure, many salespeople take their beatings but somehow recover, learn, grow, and become skilled at dealing with this situation over time—if they hang in there long enough to improve their skills at dealing with it. However, even for the ones who get through these growing pains, along with it comes the potential underlying anxiety with *every customer* who walks in. Most salespeople would do well to not only understand this, but to help prevent it by sharpening their perceptions of a customer's non-verbal cues that might indicate the presence of anxiety.

When that happens, salespeople must pause the sales process and address their customers' anxiety **before** moving to the next step. If not, the underlying effects of that anxiety will linger throughout the process and eventually get in the way of a customer saying yes to buying. This is the point where deals are lost, and too many salespeople don't realize it.

To add to all these emotions, EVERY salesperson truly wants the customer to like him/her and feel the salesperson is knowledgeable and competent at his/her job, and the main thought that never escapes him/her is the strong need and desire to get the sale or there won't be any money.

Salespeople need to find a way to harness their own anxiety and not make it evident to their customers, especially for those in the first year or two of selling. This will help them better prepare for the customer who walks in already on edge from being beaten up at the competitor down the street. Salespeople must have their antennae up and look for any emotional signal or body language cue that indicates that they have anxiety.

One major issue is that hundreds of observations of salespeople in those first few minutes have convinced me that most spend hardly any time paying attention to how they initially approach their customers. Many have no idea what they look like when they first walk up to a customer. Their pace, body language, and facial expressions all matter. I'm here to say that this is a critical step **they must take NOW** before taking even one more customer.

Salespeople should consider having someone video them approaching, greeting, and interacting with a customer in the critical meet-and-greet scenario. I have done this many times as a sales manager and trainer, and time after time, I see things salespeople need to adjust in how they approach and handle a customer in those initial few minutes. Once I play back the video, and they can see what they did, the expressions on their faces, how awkwardly they were standing and talking, they realize their discomfort was so evident, it made the anxious customer even more nervous. The result of this is a tension-filled, critical first few minutes where they have their best shot to make a good impression on the customer and they blow it because of their own nervousness and anxiety.

One of the biggest issues I have seen in these tense first few minutes is the speed at which salespeople handle this situation. Due to their nervous energy, they allow everything they do at this stage to move way too fast, which speeds things up at the exact moments they should be slowing them down and calming things.

The answer in those first few minutes: **SLOW DOWN!**

The nervous energy many salespeople have in those first few minutes often leads them to nervous actions and speeds them up when they should be taking baby steps (not giant steps). When you try to speed up an anxious customer, who doesn't want to work with a salesperson to begin with, he/she doesn't get the chance to relax, catch his/her breath, and realize that the salesperson isn't the boogie man he/she thought the salesperson might be.

The responsibility for managing this early pace belongs to the salesperson. The reason I speak so much about the salesperson's anxiety, rather than the customer (who is more important), is that the salesperson's anxiety greatly adds to the anxiety the customer already had walking in the door.

We all tend to be a little subconsciously edgy when meeting someone for the first time, but salespeople need to have an internal clock in their heads to consciously slow the process down so emotions and edginess can calm down and relax. Everyone needs to take a second and let the early moments breathe and settle in, and most salespeople lack a common sense of timing that goes into the early stages of a customer rapport-building process.

If you think about it, it's no different than meeting someone for the first time in a casual setting. If you observe it, you will see that people generally tend to be more patient with each other in this situation, letting the moment flow smoothly until they start to feel comfortable. There's no selling to take place in this situation, which can add pressure to it, and this approach DOES work if you let it. None of us needs any extra aggravation or stress in our lives, yet some customers procrastinate on entering into a shopping process because they're intimidated by whom they might end up working with along the way.

Being adept at handling your customers' anxiety comes down to making it a habit to actively look for the cues that may indicate discomfort (sometimes they are quite subtle) and then taking steps to calm their nerves so you can move forward with the selling process. It's natural for us to do it with personal relationships, so why can't we do it with customers? We certainly can.

To recap, the following list is of other key steps that need to be taken

1. Clear your head of the previous customer who might have been nasty. The next customer might be the best one you've ever worked with. If possible, take as long a break as you need to and try to empty your head (clear your mind) of the discomfort of the last customer. Start new and fresh.

2. Slow your process down in the first few minutes to let the early human fears and emotions work themselves out before transitioning to your selling system, even if the company sets a time limit for you to get the customer in front of your sales manager or product.

3. Be sure to take a *one thing at a time* approach, as that's all the anxious customer can handle in the early stages.

4. Be on guard to recognize the non-verbal body language cues that might indicate your customers' discomfort, as they will greatly appreciate it if you address that in a curious, inquisitive, human way to ease their discomfort.

5. Start from scratch with every new customer…in your mind's eye, start with a blank sheet of paper and fill in the blanks by building the comfort, rapport, and trust we ALL need to feel comfortable in a sales process to proceed naturally.

6. Remember that your customer was a person first, just like you, and you don't need to jump to another gear to get past these critical early moments. Be yourself, have fun, and enjoy the process, and the customer will relax and do the same.

7. Lastly, you must have a general interest in talking to and working with people, or salesmanship will be a greater challenge for you.

No matter how you slice it, anxiety often contributes to the real human emotions that accompany both buying and selling. Most of the time, the customer isn't going to do anything about it, as he/she will rely on the **salesperson** to be aware of it and take steps to ease the discomfort. Doing so will be the first step toward rapport and trust, vitally important in the goal of achieving a sale.

The next step in helping to alleviate your customers' anxiety and discomfort is for the salesperson to understand the type of customer standing in front of him/her, which I will review in Chapter 3.

3

Adjusting to Your Customer's Type

Of all the areas salespeople tend to overlook when working with a customer, their inability to adjust how they present their product and generally conduct themselves based on the type of customer standing in front of them is near the top of the list.

Of course, salespeople have a great deal of things on their minds when a new customer walks in the door, whether it's for an appointment or just a fresh walk-in. Working with the previous customer for two, three, or four hours and then not getting a sale can leave the salesperson with a hangover that's hard to recover from, as he/she gets ready to handle the next one. Although it's sometimes not possible, salespeople must take a few minutes after handling a disappointing sales process to catch their breath and recap that visit, especially if it didn't go well. Why? Because chances are that if it didn't go well, something was missed with the customer along the way, and they don't want to repeat the same mistake with the next one. For some reason, many salespeople choose not to do this, but it's an important step to make little adjustments along the way and avoid burning through customers by repeating the same mistakes.

Sadly, I have heard way too many salespeople blame the customers for not buying, instead of looking in the mirror at why they weren't able to secure a sale. Little things really matter, and those are the things salespeople too often blow off as being insignificant. Over the last three or four years, I have talked with hundreds of customers and was shocked at the seemingly *little things* salespeople did to ruin the chance of a sale. In the customer's eyes, those little things might just be *big* things that the salesperson overlooked.

For years now, one of the main issues I have heard from customers is that the salespeople talked too much and/or didn't listen. Others say that their salesperson didn't take enough time to understand their wants and needs, what they wanted and why they wanted it, being too focused on what he/she wanted to sell, rather than what the customer wanted to buy.

Another piece of customer feedback I have heard is that his/her salesperson sounded *rehearsed*. There could be different interpretations of this, but my interpretation of it was that too many use a *one-size-fits-all selling system*. Many companies use a selling system, and when used only as a general framework to work under, that is fine. One benefit is that this will help ensure customer-to-customer consistency and also help ensure that salespeople follow a general company philosophy that reflects the company's preferences. That is fine, but only to a point.

The problem isn't that companies use a selling system. The issue is typically with how salespeople administer it. Memorizing specific words to say that are based on psychological science can be a sensible approach. The issue is that much too often there is only a casual commitment on the part of salespeople. This results in them sounding robotic and rehearsed and repeating the same words to every customer. Some salespeople feel strongly about having the freedom to choose their own words, rather than them being dictated by the company.

All we have to do is look at our friendships or family relationships to realize that we are all built differently with different priorities, styles, and personality types, and how we prefer to interact with each other. Training salespeople to approach every customer in the same way will work with some customers but not most.

Salespeople who are committed to a company's selling system repeatedly try to put a square peg in a round hole by approaching every customer according to the selling system script. Sometimes it clicks with a customer because he/she got lucky, but most of the time, customers will walk out without buying, and it often has a great deal to do with the fact that the salesperson's approach doesn't match how he/she wants to be spoken to and sold. On top of all this, some customers are **transaction-based** and just want a good deal on something they like and couldn't care less about getting to know (or like) the salesperson. They want to save money, and everything else is secondary.

Others tend to be **relationship-based,** tending to focus less on price but more on the social experience and enjoyment of shopping. They want to connect with the salesperson, form a solid, trusted relationship with him/her, and sometimes even end up becoming friends once the transaction is completed. Each of these mentioned has a different style from the other, and trying to sell the same way to each will not work. Identifying how your customer prefers to be sold and adjusting your selling style to match that will greatly improve your chances of selling something.

With transaction-based customers, there are many different types, but every one of them wants you to get down to brass tacks quickly with pricing that's in their budget or below. Customers in this group are often willing to trade features and options for better pricing and tend to be quicker sales because they don't get excited about extra bells and whistles that extra options could bring.

In the transactional-buyer category, some of the key ones are as follows:

First-time Buyer
This is someone who hasn't previously purchased what you sell, is not educated on the product or how it's built, doesn't know the features, and doesn't know how he/she could benefit. This customer tends to be hyper-focused on the price and how it relates to his/her budget, as the initial decisions on where to stop and shop will almost always be based

on that. The best way to deal with this customer is to be an educator, communicating and teaching along the way to help him/her appreciate the value of features and options and how these could positively impact the usage.

Discount Buyer
This *down and dirty* customer is built on getting the best deal and the best price…period. He/She is not looking to build customer loyalty or a relationship with the salesperson. These customers are also the quickest buyers-in, out, and buy or not. They don't care about company reputation or warranties. They want a great price…or else.

Window Shopper (curious)
This customer is typically just a browser. He/She is willing to use your time and attention to get an education but are not typically buyers. As a real estate agent many years ago, prospective clients would often come to open houses on a Sunday afternoon JUST to get decorating ideas for their homes. Some came because they had nothing else to do and wanted to be entertained for a few hours. Quickly identify them, be cordial and professional, but cut them loose as soon as possible.

Needs-based
This customer has a specific problem to solve or a need to fill, and often represents a large number of your customer base. Salespeople must set aside their commitment to their scripted selling system long enough to recognize this customer, which will help to adjust the way they proceed with him/her. Identify the customer's needs, create a list of your products that fills those needs, and if you do it correctly, you can sell to the customer for over his/her budget if you present it on that basis.

Anger/Retaliation-based
This is a smaller group of customers, but it needs mentioning because working with them can be upsetting for even an experienced salesperson. This is the group that has been badly treated by an unqualified salesperson along the way and tends to paint with a broad brush by

assuming that **ALL** salespeople are bad and must be retaliated against. This customer takes full advantage of the saying, "The customer is always right," and enjoys verbally retaliating against salespeople for the fun of it. Many salespeople come away quite bruised from an experience with this customer, and some don't recover from it.

Then there are the **RELATIONSHIP-based** customers. There are two categories of customers who fall under a relationship-based approach: **generational and style.**

Generational Customers
If you want to make a quick assessment of the type of customer in front of you, identifying what generation your customer might fall into might be one of the fastest ways to do so. There are multiple generations of customers, and all have distinct differences. I am not going to go into each in detail here, as I did so in Chapter 10, called "Know Your Customer" in my last book, *No Trust, No Sale*, which is available on all major online book sellers' websites.

Some people don't look their age, but honestly, most of us would come close to accurately identifying the generation your current customer might be in and help you remember the tendencies and priorities of each. Doing so will give you adjustments to make in how you present your product or service to the customer in a preferred way.

As an example, baby boomers born from 1946 to 1964 prefer to work in person with their salespeople but are also savvy enough to communicate in multiple other ways, such as texting, email, or social media. They also prefer email follow-up, as that generation is still quite busy and active, even in retirement, and it's more convenient for them to do so in that way. They like to make informed decisions based on facts and research when purchasing. This is also a trust-based group that can be a referral MACHINE if you treat them correctly.

Compare that to the millennials, who tend to be laser-focused on money, almost to a fault. They often look at saving money FIRST, even if it means sacrificing a bit of quality to do so. However, they tend to have more *buyer's remorse* than any other group, often regretting the poor quality of their initial purchase after the fact. So, salespeople must be quite careful to separate the *must-do* features from the *nice-to-do* features that can raise the price of something they're interested in buying.

Drilling down on the details of each generation and how it affects their buying decision can give you a quick guide to adjust to your customer in the early stages of the customer experience and improve your chances of getting a sale.

Another way to categorize your customers and help you adjust how to sell to them is to identify their *personality type*. Whether you realize it or not, we ALL have a *type*. Some of us are analytical, and when shopping, especially for a high-ticket item, we require the salesperson to answer with specifics and provide documentation to back that up. Salespeople must realize that this customer needs to be sold in exactly that manner.

Other customers are more of an expressive type. It means a great deal to those customers that we make the shopping experience enjoyable with them. These customers would get bored with a highly detailed, technocratic-type presentation. They need to enjoy the shopping and buying process, or else they simply won't purchase.

Yet other customers are a bit of a hybrid, meaning they have shades of multiple different personality types. Connect with them better, (their basic style) and make slight adjustments in how you present and sell to them, which can be done in a way they can best relate to. Customers very much like to buy from people who are like THEM, in the same way we are attracted to and connect with our friends, especially close friends whom we would tell anything to because of how much we like and trust them.

Diane Luksis (metabolic health coach) says, "Every customer has different styles, needs, personalities, and buying triggers, and we need to adjust to that."

Ryan Meca (vice-president and financial advisor at Merrill Lynch) says, "I know that some people may be more structured and methodical than I am, but showing a true interest in the wants and needs of the person in front of you is what works best."

In all of the salespeople I have hired, trained, and coached over the years, being committed to and mastering how to identify your customers' types and then adjusting how we will sell to them is a step that so many salespeople simply don't take as often as they should. Learning how to identify your customers' types in the early stages becomes very simple and natural with practice and can improve an average salesperson's closing ratio a great deal.

Do you know who does this every day? The top 10% of the most successful salespeople. They recognize the value of taking the time to accept, study, and master this as possibly the single biggest step they took that separates them from most other salespeople who struggle to barely eke out a living every month. This group intrinsically knows how critical adding this arrow to their quiver is to up their odds of selling to even the toughest customer they face. They realize the value of being *chameleon-like* in adapting to their customer and how it could translate into a higher closing ratio and greater commissions.

Over time, implementing the ability to adjust to your customer type will become easier and more naturally work into your selling system. After a while, salespeople who commit to this tend to hone their skills and can adjust their selling style on the fly without ever noticing it. Commitment to using it, as well as practicing it, will help this evolve.

The best way to understand this is to be more aware of the times when YOU are a customer and how you felt when you were working with a salesperson and how he/she tried to sell you in a way that was uncomfortable for you. I'll bet there have been many times when you have said to yourself, *Why doesn't he do this?* Or *why doesn't he do that?* This situation is part of the reason customers come away from an encounter with a salesperson with a negative perception of him/her.

As a customer, there have been times when I couldn't wait to get away from salespeople because they tried to work with me in a way that was not a comfortable fit for me.

For the salespeople whom I have trained or coached who have truly committed to the theory of identifying the type of customers in front of them and then adjusting their style to better connect with them, most have risen to the top of their company in sales performance.

Charles Weitz, one of the salespeople (and contributors) who shared his testimonial in this book (and also someone whom I hired and trained), has completely bought into this approach. Over the years, Charles mastered this approach and grew to become the top salesperson at a nationally recognized recreational vehicle (RV) company, Alpin Haus in upstate New York, despite having no experience in selling.

Charles's customers bought from him because of the incredible connection he formed by adjusting his style to **THEM**. He is a great example by identifying the type of customer standing in front of him and being enough of a chameleon to adjust what he does and how he does it. As a result, he is more capable of achieving comfort, rapport, and trust that his customers want to have to feel okay buying from him. When rapport is built with customers in this manner, **this** type of customer has the potential to become a referral **MACHINE**, which I will discuss in Chapter 14.

The key takeaway here is that all customers come in different shapes, sizes, and personality types. The one-size-fits-all selling programs of the past simply no longer work with the savvy customers of today. Not adjusting to your customer is the most overlooked aspect of selling today, and one of the main reasons why the turnover of salespeople in industries where there is serious money to be made shouldn't be happening at the rate it is.

Just because most companies don't teach this isn't a good enough reason to not take the initiative and commit to your self-development to become proficient in mastering the connection with your customers.

Doing this also forms the foundation of the single most important aspect of selling, which is developing the comfort, rapport, and trust your customer MUST feel comfortable buying from you, which we will review in detail in Chapter 4.

4

Building A Foundation of Trust

Over the years, I have heard a variety of opinions as to when the building of trust begins with your customer, but observing salespeople hundreds of times has convinced me that it's much earlier than I ever imagined.

Some might say that it begins when you put the customer in front of your product for the first time, yet others say that it's as soon as the customer walks through the front door of your business. Although that might be a sensible start, I contend that it begins before any customer is within miles of your business. From observing hundreds of salespeople greeting customers, I believe it must start with the salesperson's belief system and commitment long before greeting customers at the front door.

Why is this so important? Over the years, numerous studies have shown that the percentage of customers who trust their salesperson is in **single digits!** This is a serious issue that must be resolved immediately. Why? When you think about it, you might realize that trust is at the heart of most of the decisions we make in our lives and not just in a sales-type situation.

It's a critical component of how we select our (true) friends, whom we want to be able to tell everything to. It plays a role in how we choose important people to take advice from, such as bankers, attorneys, and financial advisors, and it's certainly a consideration in deciding for whom we want to be employed. It's essential to us that we trust the company we work for to fulfill the promises made during the job interview. Most importantly, it eventually plays a critical role in whom we end up marrying.

I believe that most of us would agree that we strongly prefer to trust the individual trying to sell something to us as an important component in any buying process, especially if it's a high-priced, costly product, such as an RV, home, car, or even furniture.

The question is if this is such an important contributor to the sales process, then why don't companies make it a priority to train their salespeople on how to be better at it?

I have spoken to some sales managers about this and have gotten a variety of answers (and excuses). It often comes down to not having enough money in the budget and/or not having a qualified individual on the payroll who has the skills to teach others to be proficient at trust building. Others have never even given it a thought. In some cases, company leaders don't see the philosophical need to make it a priority, but it seems obvious to me that it's a pay now, pay later proposition.

I have also reviewed some of the sales systems that companies use, and I have not yet seen specific steps in any of them that prioritize building trust or teach how to do it. In implementing any selling system to build credibility with your customers, trust must not only be one of the highest responsibilities you take on but also one of the first things you strive to accomplish in those important early moments. It's a priority you must achieve, especially when it involves the anxious customers I described in Chapter 2.

Over the years, in coaching many salespeople, I typically ask them if they ever attempt to build trust in those important first few minutes of meeting a customer. Though it's often acknowledged as making sense, very few choose to do so. Instead, they try to impress customers with their outgoing personality and product knowledge. If that were true, then why do 70% of customers leave their businesses without ever purchasing anything? This doesn't appear to be working, and it's obvious to me that most don't even give it a second thought.

For those naysayers whose closing ratio is likely in the single digits, here are some great reasons why making trust-building a priority in the first 15-20 minutes is such an important priority to consider going forward.

Customer Preference

Most customers want, need, or demand to work with a salesperson they trust. Why? Because people like to buy from someone they like and trust. It's human nature. Having your customer trust you is one of the very first judgments customers make about a salesperson. It's a *vibe* they get that must *feel* right, and if it doesn't, everything else that follows will be more of a challenge. As a customer, ask yourself if you have ever purchased from a salesperson whom you did not trust at all. I bet you did not buy anything from him/her.

Get Honest Information

Whether we believe it or not, and like it or not, many customers will hold back at least some information in the early stages about what they want, why they want it, and how much they are willing to pay for it. In other cases, friends or relatives will advise them to hold back information, thinking (incorrectly) that this will give them negotiating leverage a few hours later. The anxious customer who has been the beneficiary of a previous bad experience with a salesperson is even more likely to withhold information needed to put him/her on the right product, which is hopefully in the budget.

Accept Your Demonstrations

Customers who trust you will attentively follow your product demonstration, listen carefully, and appreciate how your product will benefit them. They will not only accept your presentation about features and options but will also consider how the product will meet their needs and/or resolve their issues because they will perceive the salesperson as a trusted, knowledgeable professional.

Increase Credibility
Customers who trust you will have faith that recommendations and suggestions made will be in *their best interests* and not that of the business. This will set the stage to reduce questions later in that process because they will believe what they are being told about product features or how the product will best fit them is legitimate.

Retain Information
Customers who trust their salesperson will listen more intently and retain the information that is communicated to them during the presentation. The customers who trust their salespeople tend to pull out a pen and pad and take notes. If they do this during a presentation, that is a positive sign that trust has been built.

Pre-empt Objections
Customers who trust their salespeople will ask *smaller* questions and will ask them the questions much earlier in the shopping process, rather than bringing them up later in the form of objections while the salespeople are trying to close the deal. This also helps filter out early concerns before they fester in a customer's mind and become an emotional obstacle to buying later on.

Disregard Online Comments
Customers today, more so than ever before, are looking at online comments and a company's website before stopping in at a business, not just to look at inventory and find product preferences, but to examine feedback from other customers about their experiences. Even the nervous customer who reads concerning feedback online will quickly disregard it if the salesperson he/she is working with has built a solid rapport and trust.

Repeat Sales

Repeat customers can lead to a higher profit and a quicker sale because these customers return to the business with trust already established. They look forward to working with that salesperson again. It's one less thing a salesperson has to focus on in a return visit, which makes the second purchase much more efficient and less time-consuming.

Increase Referrals

The referral customer is typically the best and highest-profit customer because it's based on advice from a trusted friend or relative. The referral customer is also less affected by negative online comments from previous customers because he/she trusts the source of the referral. Although each new customer is somewhat of a new ball game, the salesperson can communicate with confidence based on the positive experience relayed to his/her customer by the referring partner.

As I interviewed my contributors to this book in multiple sales venues, I got a strong reaction across the board, and all of them are convinced that achieving trust is attainable with a variety of simple human actions and commitments. Here is a sample of a few of those.

Erik Betz (training & development specialist at Alpin Haus in upstate New York) states, "Building trust takes solid consistency; when you say you're going to do something, you must follow through."

Ryan Meca (vice president, Merrill Lynch) says, "Clients want to feel that I am listening to them and that I'm acting in their best interests at all times."

Adam Isabella (insurance broker) says, "You have to have enough confidence in yourself to be vulnerable enough to **really** listen to your customers."

Brian Osborn (real estate agent) says, "Just be real and honest. If customers get the perception you are just trying to get the sale closed, trust will not be built."

Bob Rose III (Warrior Performance Group) says, "If you are truly upfront and honest when they ask you something that you don't know the answer to, be honest and say that, but then go and get them the answer they need."

Diane Luksis (metabolic health coach) says, "Trust is built on sincerity." BAM! That's simple, but it hits the nail right on the head.

When you read each of these quotes, you quickly realize that all of these approaches are basic human needs that most of us greatly value in any growing relationship, whether it's personal or business-related. Though building trust is a critical step in the selling process, why do so many salespeople decide not to make it a priority, especially early in the meet- and-greet stage with a customer? This takes on even more meaning with the anxious customer.

Each of the areas I listed above does not require significant training or expertise, but they do require deciding to add them to your current selling process or system. I have not seen evidence that doing so would compromise the company's selling system in any way. It's also important to understand the risk in NOT doing this with a customer. Achieving comfort, rapport, and trust with a customer is no different than what we would normally want in growing any personal relationship or friendship. This is especially true with customers who perceive that making a purchase is more of an emotional process than a logical one, as described earlier in this book.

A study some years ago by the Harvard Business Review showed that trust is more important than price, but some salespeople have not yet bought into the concept. The question is how many customers you have to work with—spending hours with them demonstrating your product—before they walk out saying, "I want to go home and think about it," before you realize that trust should have been established. In many cases, when customers say that they don't realize until hours or, in some cases, days later, that the reason they said that is because they didn't trust the salesperson.

My good friend, Jack Daly, one of the best sales trainers in the world, says that "trust trumps price, quality, service, and company reputation." That alone is reason enough to make the decision now to include building trust in the early stages of your interactions with customers.

Earlier, I reviewed some of the things that customers expect and must have from a salesperson to lay the groundwork for trust. Remember that trust forms the foundation to truly start selling from the bottom up because it's one of the best ways to relieve the customer of the anxiety with which he/she walked into the business. It also forms the **link between your customer's intention to buy and the actual decision to buy.**

My last book, *No Trust, No Sale*, is a step-by-step, detailed plan of everything you can do to build trust. For now, here are some additional things salespeople can do to contribute to building trust with their customers. As I review these, I would ask any salesperson reading this to take inventory on whether you're currently using any of these steps or not.

1. NAIL the Greeting

Many hours of observing and evaluating how salespeople greet their customers have given me a whole new perspective on the things many salespeople tend to overlook when approaching a customer for the first time. We have all heard the phrase, "You only get one chance to make a good first impression." It is amazing how many things customers subconsciously perceive (and decide) about us in the 8 or 9 seconds it takes to approach them for a "meet & greet."

There have been numerous studies that prove that customers decide how professional we are, how confident and strong-willed we may be, how educated or knowledgeable we seem to be, whether we will be passive or aggressive, and many other things. These things set the early mood of customers in those first few minutes and show how they initially might respond to us.

2. Use The Platinum Rule
We've all heard the term, *"Treat others the way you want to be treated."* In his book called *The Platinum Rule*, Tony Alessandra teaches us to use a different and much more effective approach, which is to *"treat others the way that THEY want to be treated."* Identifying the type of person in front of you and adjusting to how you approach and speak to him/her has been one of the most amazing changes I have made with clients. I have also implemented this in my daily life with my personal friends (please don't tell them).

In many cases, we make these subconscious adjustments in our relationships, but we just don't realize it. Generally, this is a more conscious understanding and approach that goes a long way in improving understanding and communication with others.

3. Read Customer Body Language
My experience has been that all customers give off some cues in their body language, some of which are positive, some of which are negative, and yet others could be neutral. Either way, being knowledgeable about those cues, what they mean, and how a salesperson needs to respond to them is a great guide on how to proceed. This is especially true with the anxious or nervous customer, who might be less willing to communicate as openly as we might hope. It will also give a strong cue for the salesperson to be more conscious of managing the pace in those sensitive early moments.

4. SLOW DOWN!
If there is one consistent mistake salespeople make in the early stages of working with a customer, it's not finding a pace that's comfortable for the customer. My observations have proven that 75% of salespeople move way too quickly in the first few minutes of meeting a customer. As stated earlier, the last thing an anxious, nervous customer wants is a

salesperson who is overly upbeat, edgy, excited, talks too much, and is in a big hurry. Most customers prefer a calm, softer approach until early activities and conversations determine their general mood, along with a verbal pace that best fits them. The successful salesperson tends to be highly aware of the pace he/she uses in those first few minutes and adeptly adjusts that to the customer, rather than making the customer make adjustments to him/her.

Most salespeople underestimate the impact that not doing this can have on a customer and often rush right into their selling system before the customer can catch a breath. This can cause the customer to perceive that the salesperson is not necessarily there to help him/her and is trying to force him/her into an approach he/she isn't comfortable with.

Get out your highlighter and highlight this. It's THAT important.

5. Be Genuine

I am not happy to have to state this, but it needs to be said. I have witnessed numerous situations, both as a sales manager and as a customer, when a salesperson exhibited an insincere, phony approach, accompanied by a fake, manufactured smile. For many customers who can see right through this it often confirms their negative perception of salespeople, especially after they've had a prior bad experience with one. This is an immediate turn-off and gives the anxious customer a convenient excuse to leave the premises with no chance of buying anything.

6. Talk Less, Listen More

One of customers' chief concerns (and complaints) regarding salespeople is that they talk too much and don't listen to them. This is one of the quickest ways for a salesperson to lose any chance to build rapport and trust with a customer, and along with it goes the opportunity to get a sale. Stop talking and listen. Period.

Everything in this book is based directly on my hiring, training, coaching, and observing salespeople working with customers over many years.

There will be no more important chapter in this book than *this one* because building the foundation of trust is the cornerstone that makes everything else in selling possible.

It's true a salesperson *can* occasionally get lucky and be in the right place at the right time when a customer walks in with cash in hand and a determination to spend it on something. I have seen this happen. To sustain a long career of achievement in selling, everything in this chapter needs unlimited devotion and complete commitment to learn, master, and deliver superior performance, day in and day out. That's the salesperson who will be at the top of the heap every year, and one whom all others want to be like going forward.

This chapter is one I suggest that salespeople read multiple times, as it lays the foundation for everything that follows in this book. Everything in it must be executed consistently to give salespeople the absolute best chance of achieving comfort, rapport, and trust with their customers.

One more thing that I have found to be an important early step in the meet-&-greet process is storytelling. Most customers have similar goals, so the events that can happen with them really are transferable to other customers, who seem to like the knowledge that many other shoppers face the same challenges. Suggesting things that have worked well with other customers in similar circumstances are often welcomed by them, so it's advisable to share them when appropriate.

Even when salespeople successfully deploy all of the suggestions in this chapter, it is fairly normal to run into temporary snags with customers. I affectionately refer to these as the *three minutes of discomfort* when the moment requires the salesperson to take a bit of a risk by pushing back, and in some cases, mildly challenging the customer to not take a wrong turn during the shopping process. I will discuss some of those and how best to handle them in Chapter 5.

This is not as hard as you might think, but you must be more conscious of it, prepare thoughts in advance, read the customers' cues, and react to them when you see them.

5

Product Selling or Relationship Selling?

Brian Tracy, a best-selling author and highly skilled trainer on how best to work with customers, makes the point that "…if you think too much about the sale, rather than the relationship, you will neither have the sale nor the relationship" (*Sales Pitch*).

In Brian Tracy's *YouTube* video, "The Secret to Sales Success: Relationship Selling," he states that many years ago, after years of research, the Harvard Business School determined that in the 21st century, all selling would be relationship-based rather than product- based. They determined that the salespeople who could form a solid relationship with their customers would have a much better chance of earning a sale because it was based on the customer liking the salesperson and the salesperson liking the customer.

When I first started selling many years ago, I learned through trial and error (mostly error) that relationship selling was the approach that not only worked best with my personality and approach to selling, but I also achieved significantly better results. I used to go home and tell my wife, "If I can get my customers to like me and trust me, I can sell them the state of Alaska." I honestly believed that because it worked and was most effective in achieving both sales and referrals.

One thing salespeople must decide is whether they want their sales approach to be product-based or relationship-based. In many cases, the company's selling system will at least somewhat dictate this, but even if it does, each salesperson must still decide his/her approach and how he/she plans to implement it with customers.

As an approach to this, salespeople need to decide whether they feel their customers' decisions to buy are based on logic or emotion, both in a general sense and for each different customer that comes into their business. This is somewhat determined by what the salesperson is trying to sell.

Generally, decisions to buy lower-priced, everyday consumable goods are often centered primarily around need and price. In most cases, if the need is there, customers tend to make a quick decision on whether the price is acceptable or not. They either buy or they don't. If the price is too high, they will look for the same item elsewhere.

However, with more expensive, discretionary items, such as a car, an RV, a new home, and other high-ticket products, logic is absolutely a part of decision-making. However, these types of decisions are also highly emotional. When we are picturing ourselves riding in a new car or RV, living in a new home or even sitting in new furniture in that new home, one major part of the decision-making is that it has to *feel good*, or the sale doesn't happen.

When I was a sales manager and then director of employee development for a northeast RV company, many times I saw first-hand how emotions played a major part in a customer test-driving a $300,000 motorhome and how it made him/her feel sitting in that driver's seat. Logic always plays a part in a purchase like that, but emotions tend to be an overriding factor in 90% of customer decisions. Why? Because of how purchases made them *feel*. If a house on wheels is such an emotional feeling, imagine the role it could play when purchasing a brand-new home. Many of us have been there and know exactly how much of a part emotions play in major decision-making. I can certainly tell you that I feel the same level of anxiety and emotions when calling my financial manager to make a new investment.

So many salespeople today are geared toward product selling, even in the businesses mentioned above, and THAT is one reason why only 30% of customers buy from them, and 70% walk out the door without buying anything.

So, what's the message here? Where does that lead us as salespeople? The answer is that it leads us directly toward *relationship selling*, where the positives far outweigh the negatives, even though many salespeople are completely focused on product selling. The response about relationship sales appears to be unanimous within the business panel I interviewed for this book.

Ryan Meca (vice president, Merrill Lynch): "Relationship selling is much more fulfilling both personally and professionally. I've built my business over the years not by selling one particular product over another but by getting to know my customers over the years."

Diane Luksis (metabolic health coach): "I'm selling a life-transformation, which requires total trust because my customer's health is very emotional."

Adam Isabella (insurance broker): "The way things change in our business, relationships are everything. My customers want an agent that has my back and takes all the guesswork out of things."

Bob Rose III (CEO, Warrior Performance Group): "Knowledge of your product is key, of course, but if you sell yourself and build trust with the customer, you can sell anything, even if you don't know the product that well."

Erik Betz (training & development specialist): "By prioritizing the relationship, we show our customers that we're genuinely interested in more than just the sale."

Here are some other reasons why relationship selling so often comes out on top:
- Builds customer loyalty.
- Helps to sell more high-profit accessories, which increases the amount of the total sale, the amount financed, as well as the salesperson's commission.
- Promotes repeat purchases, and in less time, because a solid relationship has already been established.
- Increases the percentage of future sales at premium pricing.
- Helps customers overcome their overall dissatisfaction if technical or manufacturing issues with the product.
- Reduces objections in future business transactions.
- Increases customer referrals because the referral was given by a happy customer to another trusted friend.

Many companies have formal, written *selling systems*, and they train the salespeople to use it with customers. Some of these are highly product-oriented because their products are manufactured with exceptional quality and precision. In this case, it's easy to stand behind a product that stands alone compared to the competition. The salesperson who adds an element of relationship selling to a superior product is positioned to make a high income each year.

However, many high-standard manufacturers tend to advertise heavily on their brand quality and reputation. That's great! However, the salesperson who can top that off with a highly-crafted dose of relationship selling, even if it's not taught or required by the company, will stand out in the industry as a nationwide sales leader.

Even if the company has a fair to good product, this makes it even more necessary for the salesperson to add an element of relationship building and relationship selling to his/her sales programs. If it's difficult for a salesperson to be proud standing in front of the product, he/she can still keep his/her head high by mastering relationship-building and setting the stage for repeat sales with the customer.

Like anything else, this requires complete and total buy-in on the part of the salesperson because the techniques sometimes won't be taught by the company. Salespeople must adjust their approach from the trial-and-error of previous customer interactions. Techniques that work with some customers can also work with others. Using those, along with the techniques in this book, will help salespeople not repeat mistakes if they are committed to a step-by-step review after each customer leaves to understand and capture what worked well and what didn't.

Every interaction with a customer can teach us something about how customers think and feel, whether we sold to them or not. Failure to sell often comes with teachable moments, but successes do, as well, by recognizing the small, specific steps and approaches that worked well and repeating them with the next customer.

6

The "Three Minutes of Discomfort"

As you might expect, there can be considerable discomfort for everyone involved in a selling process. In Chapter 2, I discussed how both the fear of rejection and pressure to meet sales goals can cause anxiety in salespeople.

However, other factors are part of the process that might not rise to the level of full-blown anxiety but cause discomfort that can have a carryover effect and disrupt how salespeople interact with their customers, which could potentially ruin a deal if it's not addressed.

General discomfort with salespeople is a real but often overlooked thing, which became evident to me when I worked to improve performance and results with many of them. This can even happen with a salesperson who is generally confident when working with customers. In observations over the years, I was always able to find at least ONE cue that indicated some discomfort with a salesperson while working with a customer, especially in those first few minutes when meeting them. Many overlook this discomfort as a normal part of the job, rather than acknowledging it and taking steps to understand and improve it.

Salespeople need to be honest in identifying the underlying things that cause them discomfort and have a better understanding of them, even if they don't have total control over them. If they don't, the stress from it can be evident in their demeanor when working with a customer. The anxious customer will be sensitive and aware of anything that causes the salesperson to seem uncomfortable and will typically misread that as a hidden agenda or some other underlying threat to him/her.

Over the years, I have spoken with many salespeople who struggle with their company's selling system for various reasons. I can honestly say that I have never met a salesperson who was 100% confident in every aspect of the selling system. There's always a thing or two that they either don't like, don't support, or don't feel comfortable. When salespeople decide not to follow a selling system because they don't believe in it, they struggle when faced with customers who present any challenge at all because they're not prepared to handle it. When salespeople choose not to follow the company's guidance, they often resort to "doing it their way," which can appear disorganized and uncomfortable to the customer, and the interaction tends to drift off course with no sale.

There are other stressful situations that salespeople face daily with customers, even when they follow the company's selling system. When salespeople work with a customer who is anxious as a result of a negative experience at the company down the street, they struggle because the company didn't train them on how to handle this particular situation.

The salesperson who doesn't believe in the quality of the company's product will feel some discomfort standing in front of a customer and trying to convince him/her that the product is better than the competitors.

One of the toughest three minutes of uncomfortable moments for a salesperson is when he/she should push back when a customer falls in love and wants to purchase something that isn't right for him/her. In this case, the salesperson chooses to pass up a sure sale (and a guaranteed commission) by pushing back against a customer who wants to buy the wrong product. Contrary to popular belief, customers *don't always know* what product is best for them. I have worked with customers who want to buy something only because their neighbor has it, and they get caught up in trying to one-up them, even if it doesn't make sense for them.

There are times when customers rely on the salesperson to be both their coach and their advisor. However, if the salesperson chooses not to take the risk to push back with honest advice when it's needed, the salesperson could be blamed later on when the customer realizes the salesperson allowed him/her to buy the wrong thing.

Some customers like to take a tough guy approach and beat on salespeople just for the sport of it, and I haven't seen any company selling program that addresses this, so it's not difficult to see how badly that might turn out.

Newly-hired salespeople will likely not yet feel confident to take the risk of pushing back against a customer who is drifting away from the sales process, even though they run a great risk of wasting two or three hours of time and effort with no sale.

Each of these situations that salespeople aren't prepared to handle will be stressful unless they develop a plan in advance. Many scenarios are often similar from one customer to the next, so building solutions on how they might handle them ahead of time will prepare salespeople for issues that are likely to arise at some point. That kind of advanced planning will also help salespeople be prepared for uncomfortable moments when they have to push back.

Randy Sobel, now retired president of Sobel Associates in University Place, WA, who developed an outstanding selling system that many companies (including ours) all across the United States used, called these uncomfortable moments the "three minutes of discomfort."

What does three minutes of discomfort really mean?

Even when things seem to be going well with a customer, there are times when it becomes necessary for the salesperson to take the uncomfortable step of pushing back to honestly (but professionally) correct the customer, keeping him/her and the process on track. When an outside source gives customers bad advice about what to buy, being assertive to get distracted customers refocused, moving them away from a product they are in love with but doesn't meet their needs or budget, or in other similar uncomfortable scenarios, salespeople must be willing to take the risk to do so, but not without a well-thought-out plan in advance. If this isn't handled correctly, it can derail an entire customer engagement, and the potential for a sale will almost immediately fizzle out.

I have found this often to be the case when customers bring in (whom I affectionately call) their broke brother-in-law, who has no money, doesn't own the products they're looking at because he can't afford them, but tags along to give the customer bad advice on what to do next. For some odd reason, customers tend to follow the advice of people like this to the letter, often making the wrong buying decision or having the process fall apart due to their negative involvement. They will sometimes force their involvement in the negotiating process, even though they have no financial skin in the game, which can cause major issues for a salesperson. All of these situations call for a salesperson to pause a process, even if it's going well, and redirect the customer to get them refocused on what they're shopping for and why.

The one necessary component for this step to succeed is that the salesperson *must have previously built trust*, as outlined in Chapter 5. If trust has been successfully built, taking mildly aggressive action to redirect a customer back on track will be perceived as good advice from a trusted partner. Trust makes it easier for the customer to accept something uncomfortable from a salesperson. Not having built trust makes this a much riskier option and one that can quickly derail a potential sale.

Salespeople must also be perceptive enough to sense when the customer is beginning to lose focus, as it can happen easily and quickly. Many salespeople either miss this (often subtle) cue that the customer is drifting away from them or avoid it entirely because they don't want to upset the applecart...big mistake!

Is this uncomfortable? It certainly is, but salespeople need to be comfortable feeling uncomfortable, or a sales process can spin completely out of control.

At one time or another, we've all shopped for a high-ticket item. When customers are looking at something quite expensive, such as a home, RV, car, etc., the process can be physically and emotionally exhaustive because of the amount of money that's at stake. Doesn't it seem that after looking at two, three, or four of any of these, you start to forget what features you saw on which product? That tends to wear customers down, and not long after that, most begin to get tired, mentally, then emotionally, and finally, physically, and that's the beginning of the end, at least for that day. Allowing a customer to get off track is the start of the train coming off the tracks, so salespeople have to actively read both verbal and non-verbal cues along the way.

If you think back to when customers first walked in, even though many tried hard to avoid working with a salesperson, they always realized that at some point, they needed one to buy something. In moments when they got distracted or off track, they expected the salesperson to be a trusted partner and, professionally and honestly, get them back on track. When the salesperson didn't do that, the customers felt they had suffered poor customer service. It ended up being just one more reason for them not to buy anything that day.

In summary, salespeople have to accept that they have the responsibility of not just providing a systematic, enjoyable, informational shopping process that customers can enjoy, but they're also expected to achieve the desired results for the customer. Salespeople must accept that at times they also have to play the role of coach, which might include providing an honest opinion or push back that might be uncomfortable at the time but will lead the customer toward making the best buying decision.

Salespeople must realize that ultimately, they will be judged on performance and results, and though pushing back for three minutes might be uncomfortable or risky in a given moment, the customer will respect them later for doing just that.

Pushing back on a customer when it's necessary earlier in the process also helps the salespeople understand the authority limits they have built with the customer. This is highly valuable information that will become part of the closing approach and strategy with that customer. It's better to identify those limits earlier in the process as they can be used to hone how the salesperson may attempt to close the sale later in the process. If more work needs to be done, it's better to know that sooner, so it doesn't emerge as part of an objection later on.

One of the ways salespeople can avoid being in an uncomfortable position with a customer is to create a library of every possible situation they might encounter with a customer and prepare a basic concept of what they will do and say when each occurs. This is simply a way of having arrows in their quiver, which will help them appear smarter, be more prepared, and ultimately land them more deals. Although salespeople can't predict every situation that might come up with their customers, sitting down and recalling the ones that have come up in the past and creating strategies on how they plan to handle each one in the future will greatly improve their closing ratio when they do.

Like many other suggestions in this book, buying into this ongoing issue and taking steps to get out ahead of it is necessary to have the motivation to do the extra work to prepare for it. Frankly, it's a pay now, pay later proposition, and winging it simply does not work. Passing on the opportunity to fix this now will affect closing ratios for years to come.

To help salespeople be better prepared to handle the three minutes of discomfort, I have identified many uncomfortable situations salespeople can face each day with some suggestions to consider as a starting point. In this exercise, write down how you are handling that situation now and then how you might handle it going forward after considering the approach I suggest. The important thing here is that you walk away from that chapter with a solid idea of how you might handle each situation when they come in the future.

Doing this one exercise can help you handle uncomfortable situations that may arise in the future in a way that is better than you do currently.

7

Situational Salesmanship

I have said many times that I wish customers would be required to pass a class on how to manage a shopping process before they walk into any business or dealership and work with a salesperson to purchase a high-ticket item. Not only would they be more prepared for what was to come, but they would also be more knowledgeable, more efficient, and would likely spend their money more wisely for a product that meets their needs.

Salespeople typically deal with multiple personalities and customer types every day, and if not thoroughly prepared in advance, soon discover that a one-size-fits-all selling approach some companies use today will not prepare them to be flexible enough to adapt to different types of customers. Most of the sales systems that companies use are quite effective, but they often overlook the role that different personalities and customer objectives play in a successful transaction.

Companies that commit to funding a qualified trainer, along with sufficient funds to properly train new salespeople and provide ongoing training for existing ones, have a good chance of establishing a productive sales staff. Frankly, it's a *pay now, pay later* proposition.

Customers from different generations each have different mindsets, priorities, and goals in a shopping situation. Customers from the baby boomer generation have significant differences in philosophies and values compared to Gen-X customers. There is some crossover, but for the most part, each generation thinks and acts differently from the generation before it. The salesperson who approaches each in the same way might get lucky once in a while, but unless the salesperson adapts his/her presentation to a way that respective customers find acceptable to their generation, it will be like trying to put a square peg in a round hole.

Many customers have different personality types, as well. The expressive customers need a fun, exciting shopping and demonstration process with laughter that's not too serious or overly dependent on details. They need to have fun while shopping, and being able to decide to purchase something will be difficult. The analytical shoppers demand to have a detailed information presentation with facts and documentation backing up the demonstration. They're all business and care very little about having a fun time shopping, as their decision to buy will be based strictly on the information and data being presented to them.

All this requires salespeople to have a chameleon-like ability to adjust to the customer on short notice. That is one of the reasons why it takes a new salesperson two to three years to get his/her legs under him/her and start to consistently get customers to say yes to buying. They don't have the experience with multiple types of customers yet, so reliance is totally on the selling system taught in the initial training, whether it fits the current customer or not.

Salespeople must have at least a basic selling system around with which to operate and then make small but important adjustments to mold their presentations to the customers they're working with at that moment. Why? Because every customer is a little different than the one who just left.

Every new customer that walks in represents an opportunity to start from scratch and then shape their presentation to an approach that particular customers must have to feel comfortable buying from them.

Salespeople who aren't willing to do this are the ones who are typically out of the business in two years. Unfortunately, this often happens when salespeople are very close to figuring this out a few years after being hired, and they pass up a potentially lucrative career they might have enjoyed in sales.

With so many different types of customers out in the market, one way a salesperson can begin to make these adjustments is to create a library of each of the different situations he/she has faced with customers in the first year and develop a basic approach of how the salesperson might handle it with an on-the-spot response to the customer.

Building a library of planned *situational salesmanship* responses from prior customer experiences and memorizing them can help salespeople respond quickly with effective, well-thought-out phrases and can help deflect customers' efforts that can take them off track. Projecting every customer situation that could arise and preparing responses in advance can increase a salesperson's comfort level and confidence under pressure and help handle mild customer objections before they grow to disrupt the possibility of a sale.

Once they have initially prepared this list of situational responses, it will be much easier to adjust a word or two (on the spot) with each new customer. Planned, well-thought-out responses to expected customer statements designed to throw them off their game can also give salespeople a feeling of confidence and the ability to know what to say next under the pressure of trying to make a sale with a customer who's pushing back against their sales efforts.

One of the keys to this type of preparation is not to make the same mistake twice when a customer puts a salesperson in a bad position, where he/she wasn't sure what to do next. The purpose is that as soon as each customer leaves, whether a purchase was made or not, to immediately write down things the customer said that threw the salesperson off guard and to begin to craft a response that could be used the next time. As stated in the last chapter, over time, salespeople need to fine-tune each response so that it ends up being words or phrases they believe in and can commit to, preventing them from being caught off guard by a customer with bad intentions.

Each of these situations may vary from one salesperson to the next, and each salesperson should have basic words or phrases to handle each situation possibly encountered. Listed below are some typical situations every salesperson may face with a customer. For each one, **write what you currently say** to respond to that statement or situation. Also listed are a few alternative responses to consider, and after doing so, write how you plan to respond to each respective customer statement in the future.

1. "I'm/We're just looking"

My current response is _____
_____
_____
_____

Other possible responses are

"Well, you're in the right place to look. Let's talk about what would be perfect for you to look at, so I don't waste your time showing you the wrong thing."

"Great! What is it that you're here to see today?"

"I understand that you're shopping around.... We have a great selection to choose from. Let's talk about exactly what you're interested in, so I can show you right where that is."

"Great! Did you know that we're having a huge sale today?"

"Great! Well, that's where it starts, right? Where do we go from here?"

"I'm happy to assist you today.... Where would you like to get started?"

"Let's chat for a few minutes and find out exactly what would be perfect for you to look at today, sound good?"

"Great! Let's take a minute to make sure I have all the information I need to give you great service today, ok?"

"Ok great! Let's not worry about buying right now.... Just give me a little more information, and we'll go have some fun."

My new response is _____
_____
_____
_____

2. "This is the first place we've stopped"

My current response is _____
_____
_____
_____

Other possible responses are

"Have you looked at our website? Did anything catch your eye?"

"I'm happy that you've chosen us.... Many others have, as well, and I'm sure you'll be happy *that you did*."

"I appreciate the opportunity to show you what we have.... I'm sure that you won't be disappointed."

"That's great! Most people make us the last stop because they are very happy with how we treat them here."

"So, after shopping online, what was the deciding factor in stopping here?"

"That's great! You're a guest here, so let me show you around. Would you like a coffee, water, etc.?"

"Our marketing department tells us that most customers have looked online before stopping in. Did you find anything on our website that caught your eye?"

My new response is _____
_____
_____
_____

3. "I have no idea what I want. I just started looking"

My current response is _____
_____
_____
_____

Other possible responses are

"That's fine.... Let's spend a few minutes together and find out what's the best fit for your needs."

"Here is a great place to start.... Let's sit for just a minute to get some more information, and we'll get started."

"I understand…deciding is a process, but I can help. Let's get started!"

"Great—you don't have to decide right now. Let's talk about what's

important to you, and I'll take you right to that product."
"That's fine—did you have something specific in mind?"

"We have different models in stock. Let's talk for a minute, so I can eliminate what isn't a good fit for you. Sound good?"

"Great! Have you done any research online that can help us get started?"

My new response is _____
_____
_____
_____

4. The customer won't give you a budget

My current response is _____
_____
_____
_____

Other possible responses are

"We've got ____ of those here…did you want to start with the lowest priced model first or the highest priced?"

"Well, I can help you figure that out as we go.…What price range did you want to get started in today?"

"If you're like most of my customers, you have a rough idea of where you want to be in price. Since I want to be respectful of your budget, where did you want me to get started today?"

"We have ____ of those in the showroom, so what price range did you want me to focus on today?"

"I'm sure you both have the same goal…to find something you like in your price range, so where did you want to start today?"

"Since I will be very respectful of your budget, what is an amount that you don't want to exceed today?"

"If we started in a price range of $150/month, does that work for you?"

My new response is _____
_____
_____
_____

5. "I've/We've only got 10 minutes."

My current response is _____
_____
_____
_____

Other possible responses

"So when you say 10 minutes, does that mean you actually have to leave in 10 minutes?"

"That's not much time. What would be your expectations during those 10 minutes?"

"So, what you're saying is I only have about 10 minutes to impress you; is that right?"

"OK, sounds good…. What would be your goal for those 10 minutes?"

"That should be just enough time to talk and help me know what to show you when you come back in. Sound good?"

"Ok, so does that mean you know exactly what you want, and I should get the paperwork ready?"

(Smiling) "Now really…you only have 10 minutes?"

"That works…5 minutes for me to show you the perfect _____ , and 5 minutes for you to pay for it. Sound good?"

"That's not something that you can realistically do in 10 minutes. Do you want to make an appointment to come back?"

My new response is _____
_____
_____
_____

6. "I know what I want. I found it online, and I just want your best price for it."

My current response is _____
_____
_____
_____

Other possible responses

"So, if I give you our best price, you're willing to buy it right now?"

"I know price is important to you, but let's take a minute to make sure that it's the right product for you. Ok?"

"Situational Salesmanship"   71

"So, price is important to you. Is that what's most important to you in this purchase?"

"Sure, but how about we take a quick look at it to make sure it's the right fit for you?"

"Great that you found something that you like. If I can get some quick information from you, I might be able to find you something better for less money. Sound good?"

"Great…what did you like best about _____?"

"OK, great! What was it that you liked best about that _____?"

My new response is _____
_____
_____
_____

7. "I don't need a salesperson; I just want to go out and look at what you have."

My current response is _____
_____
_____
_____

Other possible responses are

"We like to work with our customers because our goal is to find the perfect _____ for you that's in your budget. How's that sound?"

"I'm sure your time is important to you…we have _____ of those in our showroom and lot. How about if we figure out exactly what you need, and I'll take you right to that?"

"It's important to me that you don't waste your time looking at something that's over your budget…. Let's talk for a minute, and I'll save you some time."

"I don't like working with a salesperson either, but I will be a trusted partner for you to help find something nice in your budget. Sound good?"

"You can certainly go out and look at what we have, but I know which product the sales manager is willing to make a deal on. So, is it ok if I go with you?"

"You can certainly go out and look, but some features that you don't necessarily need could inflate the price."

My new response is _____
_____
_____
_____

8. "The price is too high."

My current response is _____
_____
_____
_____

Other possible responses

"Our price is too high? What makes you think that?"

"I see that you have spent quite a bit of time researching the pricing at our competition. Have you also researched the company's integrity, service reputation, and commitment to customers?"

"I understand.... I wouldn't expect you to buy if we were way off on the price. So, let's talk about the price we would need to be at to earn your business today."

"We know that we are in the ballpark with our competition on pricing, but we would suggest that you look closely at how we stack up in service reputation and our warranty."

"Gosh, that's a little surprising to hear because we rarely miss a proposal by much, so let's give management an offer, at least one they could consider. Sound good?"

My new response is _____
_____
_____
_____

And then there's the one that we hear more than any other. If you hear this one, "it's the right product that meets their needs or solves their problem," it is highly likely that the missing link at this point is a lack of trust with the salesperson that was not built earlier in the customer visit. Often, if asked, the customer won't be able to reveal exactly what it is that he/she is uncomfortable about but most often realize later on that it was a lack of trust.

9. "I want to go home and think about it."

My current response is _____
_____
_____
_____

Other possible responses

"I can appreciate that you want to go home and think about it because it's an important decision for you, but I would like to ask what it is that you would like to go home and think about?"

"Other than price, what else are you considering as part of your decision-making process?"

"It's been my experience that when customers say that they want to go home and think about it, it's either because they're out of time or are really not interested. Which one might it be for you?"

"You would like to think it over.... Would you care to expand on that, please?"

"Ok, fine. What did you plan on thinking about? Product? Price? Something else?"

"If you were me, what would you say to convince me to buy this today?"

My new response is _____
_____
_____
_____

There could be many more possible scenarios you need to be prepared for to have a quick and natural response. The *key* here is to identify every scenario that you may face with a customer and build a bank of responses that you are comfortable with after some practice. Over time, these responses or others that you develop will be at your disposal, and you will be able to field questions or challenges at a moment's notice.

Building an information base of answers to all customer questions and responses will help you think on your feet and respond to customer questions and situations. In addition, it also helps in building credibility in other areas.

1. Your customer feels that you are knowledgeable.

2. You are perceived as a problem solver, which builds trust where the customer feels comfortable that together you can work through any challenges that may come up during the shopping/buying process.

3. You will cement the trust that you have already established.

4. You will prevent objections from coming up later in the process.

Building this war chest of questions and answers can be done quickly because they are comments that you are likely hearing now from your customers. Taking some time to recall them and planning general responses will help build confidence in handling a customer who will buy from you, as long as you respond to his/her pushback with ease.

The key is to act NOW! Don't wait. Have a sense of urgency about this, and you will be rewarded with a greater opportunity to close deals by being completely prepared for any situation in which a customer may place you.

Finally, when I was in the RV business in upstate New York as a salesperson, sales manager, and director of employee development, I worked with a great company called Sobel University from the Seattle, Washington, area. They used a principle-centered, value-based approach to working with customers that is excellent, regardless of what you sell. They used what they call word tracks where they have specific wording for salespeople to use when working with customers through the sales process that goes much deeper than I have in this chapter.

If your company doesn't currently use them, I would suggest you consider taking their courses on your own, as they can be helpful to improve your results regardless of where you are today. Randy Sobel started the company many years ago and has now turned things over to his son, Jered, who is a skilled, knowledgeable (but very relatable) trainer, who can take anyone to the next level, and I highly recommend him.

8

Collaborative **Demonstrations**

Anyone in sales now or who has been in the past will likely tell you that it is essential to have customers feel they are product experts, who know their product inside and out and can provide a powerful demonstration to prove it. Most companies do a decent job of training their salespeople to have adequate product knowledge, at least good enough to stand in front of their customers. Product knowledge is often the thing most salespeople lean on to build customer interest, loyalty, and trust, but too often, this approach comes back to haunt them later in the process.

Before a customer will be actively receptive to listening to what a salesperson has to say about the product, he/she must trust the salesperson. All too often, a major flaw in the approach is that the salesperson rushes past those early comfort-building, rapport- building, and trust-building stages to hurry customers in front of the product, under the false impression that the excitement of that will overcome any anxiety the customer might have walked in with. It's true most customers are truly excited about getting in front of the product they came in to see, but as stated in earlier chapters, NOT UNTIL they have achieved solid comfort with the salesperson.

For their product presentation to be effective and meaningful with the customer, salespeople must have established the customers' reasons for stopping there to begin with, whether it's to fulfill a need, solve a problem, or both. They also must have a clear picture of the customers' preferred budget and the budgets they might be willing to go to for the perfect product. Without question, if the salespeople don't build trust *first*, the customers will hold back honest feelings about what they want, why they want it, and how much they're willing to pay for it. In addition, anything the salespeople say about the product won't be seriously considered because the customers do not have full faith it's being revealed with the best interests of the customer in mind. *All* salespeople must understand that every customer who walks in will have some level of anxiety that must be addressed before any product details can be successfully passed on to the customer.

Once trust is established, it will be easier for the customer to accept that the information being communicated will be done to show that it will benefit him/her and his/her wants and needs. Even if product information is communicated on a timely basis, the trap that many salespeople fall into is to spout off one product feature after another, trying to impress the customer with such a great number of beautiful features and benefits, there is just no way the customer will not want to buy it—WRONG!

After listening to (and hopefully writing down) all the reasons why a customer wants to look at a particular product and then prioritizing which of those needs are most important to the customer, salespeople must then transfer that information to their presentation. All too often this doesn't happen because the salesperson is too busy listing one feature after another, after another trying to overwhelm the customer with this massive list of goodies but not directly relating it to each particular problem the customer needs to solve or needs to fill with that feature.

In this situation, too many salespeople use up all the oxygen in the room, overwhelming the customer with so many beautiful features that only an idiot wouldn't be willing to immediately put a down payment on it.

Again, WRONG. The presentation must be a collaboration with the salesperson slowing down to not only identify the next feature, but also directly relating it to a problem it solves or a need it fills that was mentioned earlier by the customer. It's not a presentation; it's a discussion.

To truly personalize the experience of the demonstration, the salesperson must make the customer an active participant. Each feature must be presented in a way that not only emphasizes the exciting innovation or advantage over the competition that it offers, but the salesperson must take the time to illustrate the benefit to the problem or issue the customer mentioned earlier.

If a customer is looking for a new car primarily for a quiet, comfortable ride on long trips to other states, the salesperson must point out the special tread on the tires that exactly supports that need, as it's built for smooth and ultra-quiet travel down the road. The RV buyer who must have a full outdoor kitchen because he/she doesn't want to smell up the cabin with an odor of bacon grease must have a slow, step-by-step presentation of a breakfast-building outdoor kitchen that makes every step in that process easy and within arm's reach of the cook.

To build a collaborative presentation when collecting all the reasons why a customer is looking for a new car, RV, or whatever, the salesperson must be careful to prioritize which needs matter the most. The salesperson must have a clear understanding of what must-have and what are nice-to-have features and benefits. If not clear as to which the customer's priorities are the highest, questions must be asked and answered for clarification.

When giving a product presentation, too many salespeople do the walk-around in a convenient way, like starting at one end or the other and walking around in a step-by-step manner. This must be adjusted to begin with the top three to five highest priorities *first*, followed by the secondary priorities, and then, finally, all other features that have some value but don't necessarily solve a need or problem. If the presentation is sequenced in a way that coincides with the highest priority the customer needs or wants, the sale should be 90% closed after those are presented.

This is how the perception of VALUE for their money is processed in the minds of most customers. Every problem they came in to solve has been completed right before their eyes. Solving the wants and needs for customers help them justify the cost in their minds, and closing them on price will be easier because they will be getting everything they are paying for.

Too many salespeople focus on the bells and whistles that a typical customer might be excited about, but each customer has different wants, needs, and priorities. As a result, the presentation must be personalized not only based on the current customer's needs and wants, but also on *why* it is wanted. However, this can only occur after a successful meet-&-greet where comfort, rapport, and trust have been solidly established.

Focusing on how and why key features will solve a customer's needs and/or wants will improve a salesperson's chances of proving value over price. This will help refocus the customer away from the price so it doesn't become an obstacle to buying later on.

The other thing to keep in mind here is that over the last five years or so, there has been a significant increase in the level of pre-visit research and information gathering that customers now do on the internet before they walk in the front door. Customers today typically spend the time and effort narrowing down what they want and eliminating what they don't want long before they walk in the front door. Then they expect the knowledgeable salesperson to put them in front of the product that is perfect for THEM and not the last customer who was there. The general popularity of product features is meaningless to every customer and must fit into each customer's personal needs.

In terms of the order of showing products, once a salesperson gets his/her customer's budget, I highly recommend that salespeople *start with the lowest-priced product* in the customer's budget and move up gradually in price based on the customer's feedback. Here's why....

One of the biggest fears customers have is that the salesperson will try to sell them something that is over their budget or more than they were willing to spend. This is a concern that customers have been sharing with businesses for many years. To prevent this, show the customer the lowest-priced product first, even if you know that it lacks some of the important features the customer said were important to him/her during the information-gathering stage of the process. This does three things.

> 1. It helps the customers realize that if they want to buy something at the low end of their budget, they will have to go without some features that they were interested in and that they likely won't be able to have all the features they want in their current budget.
>
> 2. They will have more appreciation of the value of the features they feel they need and a better understanding of why they will need to pay more for them.
>
> 3. They will be much more willing to *bump themselves* up in price to get what they *really* want and have the features that will solve their problem or meet their needs. Once they become more willing to pay more on their own, the fear that the salesperson might try to sell them something that is above their budget tends to go away.

Starting with a product that barely meets their minimum needs sets them up for being more receptive to spending more later. It also resets their value versus price perception that might make it possible for them to be more receptive to buying a more expensive (and potentially more profitable) product than they originally intended.

As the salesperson moves the customer from product to product, it's important to take just a few minutes after each to recap what they liked and disliked, which helps keep them clear-minded and not confused as he/she looks at more products. It also helps the salesperson with what product to show next because they're getting up-to-the-minute feedback about how the customer is feeling. This approach is especially helpful when showing high-priced products like homes or RVs.

In conclusion, none of this will take place *unless* the salespeople have built a solid foundation of trust, and the salespeople will not earn the right to proceed as they wish in a way that can benefit them. One of the single biggest mistakes salespeople can make is to rush the customer in the early stages to get in front of their product without making trust-building a key priority in the first ten to twenty minutes of meeting the customer. It's a pay now, pay later proposition, and the sooner salespeople buy into this, the sooner their closing ratio will move up versus other salespeople on their staff.

9

Preparing for Objections

A great deal of salespeople perceive objections as the elephant in the room, the monster lurking behind the curtain ready to spring out and attack them and ruin a shopping process that was going great and just when the customer was on the verge of caving in and buying something. In its simplest form, objections are a moment of doubt, hesitation, or, in some cases, fear. They're just asking themselves, "Do I *really* want to do this?" Yet, so many salespeople start spiraling, explaining, defending, and overreacting at a level where they give oxygen to the customer's momentary second-guessing instead of staying calm, taking a breath, and believing in what they did for the three or four hours that led up to it.

Objections are often a key—and with some customers—a mandatory part of the sales process, starting from when the customer walks in until he/she leaves, regardless of whether a sale is made or not. In many cases, whether objections prevent a sale depends on how the salesperson handles and resolves them, regardless of whether they are real or perceived by the customer.

However, whether big or small, when objections arise, they can significantly impact a customer's emotions and attitude, influencing not only his/her perception of the product being considered but also, most importantly, the customer's judgment of the salesperson's knowledge, ability, and competence. If the salesperson isn't clear and concise in his/

her product demonstration, customer confusion can create an objection that can disrupt an otherwise positive sales process.

In some situations, customers may voice an objection to establish a negotiating position, and others may not feel comfortable purchasing something unless they state an objection to challenge their salesperson to earn the right to sell them something.

Regardless of how they emerge, managing customer objections is a key component in any sales process, which requires them to be ready for every possible scenario, so they don't get caught off guard and negatively affect their credibility as viewed by the customer. Unfortunately, many years of training, observing, and coaching salespeople have proven that too many go through a sales process *wishing and hoping* that no objections will surface, and they will earn an easy sale. However, there is a much more effective approach and one that can immediately increase a salesperson's closing ratio, and that is *preparation*.

Preparation

Instead of battling objections as they happen, I have always taught salespeople to anticipate what might be coming and to reduce the odds of them happening earlier in the sales process. If you think about it, the typical objections are often similar from one customer to the next, so it's completely reasonable to consider all the possible objections **in advance** and prepare basic responses that can be memorized and called upon when needed.

Once solidly memorized, it's easier for a salesperson to quickly adjust each to fit the specific customer objection for that customer. This will increase a salesperson's confidence level to handle them and not be intimidated when done because the salesperson will have more arrows in their quiver to answer quickly with previously established responses.

It's also sensible to understand what **causes** objections in the first place because they can play a pivotal role in changing the direction of a sales process on a moment's notice. All too often, many of these are created *by the salesperson* without ever realizing it. Here are some examples.

Relieve Anxiety Early

In my first sales book, *Know Your Customer*, I discussed knowing your customers' day to help alleviate the natural anxiety some customers bring to a sales business, caused by the normal things we all deal with in a day. When I was a salesperson years ago, I experienced real-life situations where customers would walk in the front door with obvious anxiety about something based on what they said and their body language. After helping them relax and feel comfortable, they often revealed that something upsetting had happened shortly before arriving.

When you think about it, these things happen to all of us at one time or another, and we all handle them differently. When it happens just before walking into a place of business to consider purchasing a high-ticket item, it can take its toll. It also puts the salesperson in an uncomfortable position.

Here are just a few of the real-life customer incidents I had to handle when I was selling RVs.

- Just got a speeding ticket one mile from our business.
- Had a major argument with her husband on the phone in the parking lot.
- Just got a phone call that a son got suspended from school for getting in a fight.
- Found out that a friend just received a cancer diagnosis.
- Moments before walking in, a wife received a phone call that her husband had just been laid off.

Believe it or not, there are more, and those are just a few of life's typical, stressful moments that can emotionally alter a customer's feelings and reduce the possibility of a sale at any moment. In most cases, these things are none of a salesperson's business, but when the customer communicates them to a salesperson, they become a part of the "meet & greet" process, and additional discussion (or action) needs to take place before proceeding. This may include rescheduling or (at the very least) taking more time to be a friend with sincerity and listening skills to get customers back into the frame of mind to be productive while on a sales visit.

At times, getting into the shopping process is not salvageable, and it needs to be rescheduled.

It's obviously not appropriate to pry into a customer's personal life, but customers are people, too, and in vulnerable times, sometimes they just need a friend or a sympathetic ear, and that might happen to be a salesperson at a particular moment in time. Let's face it. We've all had stressful moments in our lives. When this happens, the sales process must hit the pause button, and it becomes a moment-to-moment assessment of when (and if) to start it back up.

The Product Doesn't Meet the Customer's Needs

In the early stages of a "meet & greet," most salespeople are determined to make a great first impression and want to impress the customer with their knowledge and expertise so the customer will perceive them as professional and competent. That's completely understandable. However, as a result, the average salesperson *talks way too much* and misses valuable information that the customer is trying to communicate.

Keep it simple in the first few minutes: talk less, ask questions, listen, and make notes. Confirm what you're hearing often with a nod or comment, and ask for clarification when it's needed. The importance of this is often overlooked because every detail matters. It's not just what they want, but why they want it, how they plan to use it, and what they're willing to pay for it.

The more information a salesperson can transfer in those early stages, the less chance there will be for an objection to surface later.

Diane Luksis (metabolic health coach) says, "To prevent objections, focus on effective discovery. Take more time to understand your customers' goals, concerns, and priorities. Then you tailor your solution in a way that can naturally address their doubts *before* they come up."

The salesperson who isn't actively listening runs the risk of putting the customer in front of the wrong product, which virtually assures that it will arise later in the form of an objection. Here are some missed opportunities that can raise the odds of objections arising later.

Didn't Nail Down a Budget "Range"

Getting the true budget from the customer is harder than most think, especially when salespeople are trying to get that number before they have built comfort, rapport, and trust. Attempting to get the customers' budgets too soon is a mistake, as many either intentionally give a number that's lower than reality or have been advised to do so before they come into the business.

Also, most salespeople are typically satisfied with getting just one budget number from their customer. Too often, they fail to ask one more question that determines if they are willing to go to a slightly higher budget for a product that is perfect in every way. So, it's important to get a preferred budget but also a *maximum dollar amount the customer would consider for the product* that meets every need or want when walking through the door.

Doing this brings additional products into consideration because the salesperson is now working with a budget range instead of just one number. It also reduces the odds of a price-related objection arising later.

Missed Body Language "Cues"

Asking well-thought-out, specific questions will be enough to get all the information a salesperson needs to find the perfect product that fits the customer's budget.

However, the perceptive salesperson will also pay close attention to the customer's non-verbal clues and body language to ensure that it complements the words he/she is saying. If the customer is saying one thing but illustrating uncomfortable body language that contradicts that, the perceptive salesperson must ask follow-up questions to confirm that what the customer said is acceptable to him/her. Just like when we're talking to family or friends, some of the negative cues include tone of voice, as well.

If it's stated in a soft, curious manner, it's fine for a salesperson to say something like, I'm hearing what you're saying, but you seem a bit uncomfortable…do we need to talk a bit more about your answer?" Rooting out discomfort early on will prevent it from resurfacing later as an objection.

Proceed In a Way to Ensure the Customer is Comfortable

Many companies have a selling system they use with their customers, and although they vary from company to company, most sound a bit robotic, depending on how they are delivered. To deal with this, I have always taught salespeople to **announce** what is coming next to the customer and then *ask for his/her approval* to continue.

A huge customer fear (and often misconception) is that he/she is afraid the salesperson might sneak something by him/her. This can be easily prevented by announcing what you plan to do next and asking if it's ok with him/her. Asking something like, "Would you prefer that we start looking at products that are on the lower end of your budget first or the higher end?" This is a good way to start. Every time you want to change gears and change direction, be sure to announce it to the customer first and ask if he/she is comfortable with that. Then get his/her commitment to continue.

Doing this should remove the fear that you might be up to something suspicious and will complement the feeling of comfort and trust that was built earlier. Customers are much more comfortable when they know what is to come and that there are no secrets in the salesperson's plan that day.

Confirm that the Decision Maker is Present

There are different points of view on this, but confirming if the decision maker is present is an important one.

Far too many salespeople spend hours working with customers, and when trying to close them, they discover that they aren't the final decision maker, causing most everything that came before it a waste of time. Some sales managers and coaches like to ask that question near the middle of the process, but it's my position that it must be discovered in the early stages. There are two keys:

1. **When** to ask
2. **How** to ask

When to ask—This should be clarified as early as possible, but the salesperson must achieve comfort, rapport, and trust first. The customer must answer questions willingly and give details before asking if he/she is the final decision maker.

How to ask—Again, with comfort, rapport, and trust in place, it's completely fine to say, "Are you the person who can approve a final purchase, or will someone else be helping you decide to purchase today?" If neither buyer is present, then the salesperson should consider rescheduling or getting the second buyer on the telephone to be sure his/her needs and wants are a part of any product demonstration.

Comfort, Rapport, and Trust are a MUST

Finally, no process that transitions from "meet & greet" to product demonstration should NEVER move forward UNTIL comfort transitions into rapport and rapport transitions into trust have been successfully established.

Hundreds of observations of salespeople have proven to me that THIS is the point where more deals are lost than any other in a sales process, even more so than trying to get the customer to buy the wrong product.

Customers come to a business to look at their product, and they are excited and can't wait to go do it. They're often anxious and in a hurry, which most salespeople will sense when they walk in, and too many salespeople succumb to that urge and rush their customers in front of their product before other necessary things have been established.

The best approach to take in those early stages is to (once again) **SLOW DOWN!**

Salespeople tend to get very excited to have new customers who have the potential to turn into a sale (and a commission). The customer is also usually happy and excited to look at their potentially new shiny whatever that they might be able to take home with them. So, everybody is excited, but everybody falls into the trap--one that will cost him/her both a sale three hours later because all this excitement tends to affect the ability to listen to each other.

To avoid this, being able to establish a reasonably slow pace is the first big test every salesperson must pass before jumping into his/her company's selling system with each customer. It's also the first test needed to be passed to prove that the salesperson will control the process, not the customer. It's not openly discussed, but everyone involved feels it. Whenever a customer dictates the pace of the shopping process is often the exact moment when the salesperson gives up any control over his/

her selling system and how the customer participates in it.

It's also important to understand what you're offering the customer and why to prevent objections. Adam Isabella (insurance broker) says, "For the most part, objections come from not understanding what you're offering the customer and why. By taking those extra steps, the customer will understand exactly what he/she is buying and why."

To recap, it's time for the tail to stop wagging the dog when it comes to objections. Salespeople need to buy into why taking steps to *prevent* them, which will be significantly easier than *dealing with them later*, when the decision to buy or not buy is at stake for a customer. This creates unnecessary stress and plays a major role in reducing the chance of a sale happening. It also directly contributes to a much more enjoyable and less stressful shopping process for both the salesperson and the customer.

The final takeaway is that extra steps MUST be taken early in the sales process to ensure that your customer is comfortable, or he/she will use that as an excuse not to buy later. Being committed to preventing objections in the early stages will decrease the odds of having to deal with them later. As a result, there are fewer emotional barriers standing in the way of closing the deal.

10

Closing the Sale

You have successfully made it through the "meet & greet," selected a great product for the customer, and completed an award-winning product demonstration. You have also implemented steps to prevent any objections. So, you're done, right?

Not so fast. Now comes the hard part, the most important part, and the reward for all your hard work, which is to get the customer to say "*Yes,*" and hand you a credit card for the down payment. This is the point where far too many salespeople rush the process of asking for the sale. In some situations, that timing works just fine, but in many others, additional groundwork needs to be laid before trying to close the sale.

There needs to be a last-minute checklist that you must ensure you have completed before deciding to close your customer. Having completed this checklist before attempting to close your customer will reduce the chance of needing to close him/her multiple times, which is stressful on both the customer and salesperson. This list is as follows.

> 1. You have solidly built comfort, rapport, and trust.
>
> 2. You have actively listened to the customer's desires and put them in front of a product that achieves both, which is comfortably in his/her budget.

3. You have confirmed the customer's intentions to buy.

4. You have completed a collaborative product demonstration that solved their stated needs and wants and focused more on value than price.

5. You have accurately determined who the decision maker is.

6. You have taken steps to pre-empt any objections (or have addressed them when they arose).

Before attempting to close the customer, there is one step I have been recommending for many years, and that is to develop a "Why buy from *your company name*" one-page flyer that can be handed out just before asking your customer for the sale.

This document can be used to illustrate the competitive advantages that your company has over the competition and can lay the groundwork for your close. Some of these things might have been included in your product presentations before this, but handing out something like this recaps all the company benefits in one package and can be impressive when it precedes your closing approach. It can also be laminated to add some gloss and professionalism.

When I was a sales manager at a top 50 RV company located in upstate New York, we developed a value-added flyer that worked like a charm for us. On the next page are some examples to help get you thinking about what your company offers.

WHY BUY FROM XYZ RV?
(Sample)

- RV business "Top 50 Dealership in the U.S. out of 2,800 dealerships."

- RVDA voted Best Dealership in the U.S.

- A+ rating with the Better Business Bureau.

- 70,000 square foot State-of-the-Art facility.

- RV "Warranty Forever" Program.

- Over 400 RVs from which to choose.

- Priority RV Network member.

- Certified Service Technicians.

- 22 Bay Service Shop.

- Gated Winter Storage.

- Two free annual roof inspections for our customers.

- Voted "Best Place to Work" in upstate New York.

Developing, handing out, and reviewing a document similar to this just before asking for the sale identifies significant competitive advantages versus your competition. It also helps to lay the groundwork for your attempt to close the deal. Some may choose to hand it out at the beginning of the customer visit to get off to a great start, but something like this can be highly successful as a lead-in to closing the deal because it was a recap of positives over our competitors that helped to solidify your customer's mindset in preparing for our asking for the sale.

A key piece of closing is to create a library of words and/or phrases in advance to use in closing, regardless of the circumstances, so you are prepared to close a deal in any situation. This list should be fine-tuned over time based on the success or failure of each phrase in live situations. Some are as simple as just a few words, while others are more complex.

The key, over time, is to build a core list of dependable closing questions that fit you, reflecting your typical speaking style and approach to closing a sale, so they sound natural to your customer.

To help you get started, the following is a list of closing phrases to help you craft how to speak to your customers in each situation you may face. You can use them or modify them as you wish. They are divided into two categories: one list is to be used to ask for the sale, while the second list is assumptive closes, where you feel the sale is done and are just confirming it. The third list is where the customer is interested but hesitating.

"Regular" Closes
Pretty much everything that you wanted – is this the right one?
What do you say? Ready to fill out paperwork?
Is this the one for you?
Ready to make it yours?
Are you ready to take the first step?
This will look good in your driveway, won't it?
Is there any reason to wait?

What do you think? Should we start the paperwork?
So, let's get your credit card and make it yours! Sound good?
Shall I write this up?
Should we get this ordered?
Is it a go?
Ready to move forward?
Why not write it up now, pending your spouse's approval, to make sure that no one else buys it on you?
Should we put your name on it?
OK, let's wrap this one up. Sound good?
Is this THE ONE?
Shall we make this a reality for you?
Time for paperwork?
Well, what's the word?
Well, have you folks made a final decision?
Well, you've got our best price on this. Can we offer you a discount on some accessories?
I feel like you deserve this, don't you?
Is it a YES?
Got your checkbook with you?
Will you be taking it with you, or do you want it to be delivered?
Are we all set then?

"Assumptive" Closes
Do you want to pick it up on Monday or Tuesday?
Ok! I'll get the paperwork started!
How soon can I have it delivered?
Which day is best to deliver it? Monday or Tuesday?
What color would you like me to order?
It suits you perfectly; let's get it ordered.
I'll get the paperwork, so we can write it up.
How soon do you want to be enjoying this?
OK! Let's get you on the books!

"Interested" Closes
I can tell that you're excited. What's preventing you from moving forward today?
Other than price, what's causing your hesitation today?
You've been so excited all day. Has anything changed?
Well, you love ___, and ___. What's holding you back?
I have been so happy to find the perfect _____ for you, but you seem a bit hesitant. What's going on?
Of all the ____ we've looked at today, you seem so excited about this one. And we know it's in your budget, yet you seem a bit hesitant.
I seemed to feel your emotions change when we got to ____. What caused that?

Hopefully, the list above will get people thinking more about how to craft closing statements in every possible situation. Everyone needs to have a series of different closes that can be memorized and easily adjusted in the final minutes after hours of hard work.

After working with many salespeople over the years, I'm shocked at how many do not have **go-to closes** that work best for them. Trying to close the sale can be awkward, *especially* when there is something the customer is hung up on, regardless of how small. Deciding to say yes to buying is an emotional moment for most customers, and it has to *feel right*. When it doesn't, a customer's body language will typically tell the story of an obstacle lurking.

It's at THAT moment when the salesperson must adjust *if* and *how* to ask for the sale. Although it sometimes takes multiple closes to get a customer to say yes, the first time he/she says no to buying is the hardest emotional obstacle to overcome. When asking for the sale the first time and it doesn't work, time must be spent finding out why.

A key obstacle many salespeople struggle to get over is when the customer rejects the initial attempt at closing, which often affects them emotionally as well. Salespeople must keep in mind that *"No"* very often means "not right now," so there is still life left in the deal.

Bob Rose (CEO and Founder of the Warrior Performance group in upstate New York) says, "The sale really starts when the customer says no, so be the BEST listener and react with FACTS. Don't be afraid of rejection. Remember, the customer might have a fear that you may say no to his/her offers, as well."

In addition, the salesperson must be convinced that the product he/she is trying to close really IS the best one for that customer.

Realtor **Brian Osborn** from Oasis Realty Collective in Myrtle Beach, South Carolina, says, "I will go over all the positives as to why a property makes sense for a client, but the client must have expressed that it feels right." Therefore, a verbal affirmation, backed up by complementary body language, must be in place before attempting to close the deal with a customer."

Ryan Meca, V.P. from Merrill Lynch, adds, "I don't have certain phrases I always use, but I always make it a collaborative decision. I might say something like, 'I think I have a good understanding of what you're looking to accomplish, and I feel like I can really help you. Do you think it's a good idea to get started together?'"

To increase the chance of closing any sale, salespeople must not only be flexible and adaptable, but they must also commit to continuous improvement to prepare themselves to close customers in ANY situation. One major way to do so is to develop and memorize closing statements that they can use in any situation. They can do so by using the closing statements listed in this chapter, writing their own, or using a combination of both.

In addition, developing a list of value-added advantages their business can provide versus their competition will help customers use that information to find the best overall deal in the decision making process.

11

Legendary Follow-Through

Some things in selling are beyond the control of salespeople but affect how much money they can make, like the quality of their product or the amount of advertising money their company is willing to spend to attract customers to their business. One *critical* component of their success that is largely within their control is the level of follow-through they exhibit with their customers.

This entire book is devoted to the steps salespeople must take to capitalize on the trust they have built with customers and turn that into the ultimate goal: getting the sale. Although there are no guarantees when it comes to working with customers, following each of the steps in this book will go a long way in determining whether that hard work will result in a customer eventually saying yes to buying something.

To be fair, many salespeople have decent follow-through skills. They know it's important and, for the most part, do a pretty good job at doing what they said they would do when they said they would do it. But is that good enough? No, it's not because the guy down the street will be doing the same thing.

Salespeople need to understand that to stand out against the competition, they need to do things at a level that no one else who competes with them is doing. And following up in a *legendary* manner is one of them. It's something that starts the moment the customer walks through the front door.

During customers' visits, it's typical that they will ask a question that the salesperson doesn't know the answer to. One of the best ways to start to build credibility for great follow-through in this situation is to say, "I don't know the answer," to a question. What? Far too many salespeople who don't know the answer to a question tend to make one up to sound smart, but guess what? Most customers can see right through that because that is one of the customer's biggest fears: being lied to.

First of all, saying, "I don't know," to a question is very honest, but what you do immediately after that is the key. The best way to handle this is to say, "I don't know the answer to that question, but I will get hold of someone who does, and then we'll both know."

When I first started in RV sales, there were many product questions that I couldn't answer, so I prepared a list of resources on every area of the business I could call on at a moment's notice and did exactly that. I would call my representative at the respective manufacturing plant, put the phone on speaker, introduce the customer to him/her and proceed to ask the question. Then the customer had the opportunity to ask additional questions if needed, and the customer got answers. I did as well (for the next time). The customer felt respected when he/she got to talk to someone in Indiana, who was at the plant where the RVs were being built, and was very grateful that I made that connection for them.

There were other times when I didn't know the answer to a question, and I immediately got someone on the phone to answer it or put someone in front of the customer, whom I introduced and got the answer. After multiple times of doing this, the customers had NO issue that I didn't know the answer to some of their questions and viewed me as their *answer man* because I immediately followed up to get someone who could answer their questions. It showed respect with high-quality follow-through. No! It was LEGENDARY follow-through.

From that moment on, everything that followed was easier because I built credibility in how I handled the answer to "I don't know." Most salespeople struggle to admit when they don't know the answer to a question, but in reality, I built credibility as an honest broker for them.

This worked so well that as I became more knowledgeable about the products we sold, I sometimes would say that I didn't know the answer, EVEN IF I DID KNOW IT, so I could bring in other resources in the name of superior customer service. Customers grew to know that even if I didn't know the answer, I had the power to initiate an immediate response from others, which they viewed as a high sign of respect. You need to set your ego aside to make the best business decision for your customer.

One takeaway not to be missed is that from respect comes TRUST. Trust is one of those things where if it is not established, the odds of getting that sale decreases substantially, as I have stated throughout this book. Legendary follow-through is one way to solidify trust. Making trust-building a priority and implementing some of the techniques, including legendary follow-through, allows salespeople to stay calm and confident, allowing the other parts of the customer process to flow smoothly.

We all know that many customers tend not to make a decision to buy something on their first visit. Even legitimate buyers often say, "We want to go home and think about it," and there are many reasons for that. With many customers, the word "*No*" doesn't exactly mean that; it means "not right now," as stated in an earlier chapter. Not buying on the first visit is often the way some make purchasing decisions, and in many cases, they don't even know why. When this happens, this situation requires a salesperson's timely follow-through, but this is the point where many potential deals just fade away.

There is a great deal of research on why salespeople don't do a good job of following through with their customers in this situation. However, there are statistics that support the fact that only 2% of sales are made on the first visit, and on average, it takes seven to ten visits for a sale to take place. Yet, 44% of salespeople give up after one follow-up call, and only 12% make three or more follow-up calls—not exactly legendary. What makes this more frustrating is that 42% of customers surveyed said that they're more likely to purchase if their salesperson calls them back, especially if it's on the day and time they initially agreed to (Cardone).

Understandably, some customers do not like emails or phone calls once they have left the place of business without buying something. This is especially true when trust and legendary follow-through haven't been established. When these aren't solidly in place, the customers start to feel harassed when the person they've worked with starts doing *"that salesman thing,"* driving them crazy and calling four or five times a week, trying to get them to answer the phone. When this happens, a deal is highly unlikely.

However, the customer who trusts his/her salesperson and consistency in follow-through will be significantly more receptive to receiving phone calls and is also more likely to call back.

Frankly, there needs to be some self-accountability here. Although this may sound harsh, being able to follow up is a core *decision* salespeople need to make if they choose to be in the sales field. Consistently following through is not luck, fate, or karma; it's a DECISION. Frankly, anyone not all-in on this should consider leaving the business because his/her chances of being successful are exceedingly slim.

Let's back everything up a bit. To build legendary follow-through for today, it must start at the end of the day—YESTERDAY. One of the last things salespeople should do before going home for the day is to prepare their list of follow-throughs that must commence *as soon as they walk in the door* tomorrow. Too many salespeople start to think about what they need to do each day at the beginning of the day. That's TOO LATE. By the time we arrive at work each day, we say hello, have a coffee, and check for messages and emails; hours have passed, and the day is already half over.

To truly craft a solid plan for the next day, salespeople must also have a format in which to do that. All aspects of follow-through must be clearly outlined, including tasks to complete, emails to send, calls to make, appointments to prepare, and any necessary internet information to research. Relying solely on your memory often doesn't work, as things do come up. Many different formats can be used, whether handwritten or electronic. Next is a one-page, simple follow-up sheet I have been using for thirty years. Copy it if you like, adjust it, or develop your own and use it as a guide going forward.

SELLING FROM TRUST

Name: _____
FOLLOW UP FOR TODAY
_____   ___/___/___

TO-DO

_____

_____

_____

_____

_____

_____

_____

CALLS & EMAILS

_____

_____

_____

_____

_____

_____

_____

APPOINTMENTS TODAY

_____

_____

_____

_____

_____

INTERNET RESEARCH

_____

_____

_____

_____

_____

I just go to my local printer and have him create 5 1/2" X 8 1/2" pads of 50 each, which fit nicely on my desk for a very reasonable cost. I have had hundreds of people copy this and implement it for their use, but if you prefer something different, that's fine as long as you have *something* to use as a guide to manage your follow-through performance each day.

I can tell you that in the early days of my career, my follow-through wasn't the priority it should have been, and I took some lumps for that. However, once I made follow-through the single highest priority each day, I became known for it, and if people mentioned my name, others would often say, "He has the best follow-through I have ever seen." I built the credibility of my *word* as a corporate executive, sales manager, and trainer over the years, based on follow-through. The impact of a commitment to having legendary follow-through won't just have a massive impact with your customers; it will do the same for the perception of your superiors and peers alike.

When you think of follow-through, what comes to your mind? To me, it's simple. It's doing what you said you would do when you said you would do it. You have heard the saying, "Your word is your bond." Having legendary follow-through forms the foundation on which others can trust you. When you combine honesty with a commitment to follow-through, that forms a powerful basis on which your reputation and personal credibility can be built.

When you look closer at how customers perceive salespeople, just imagine what a powerful role that could play in changing your customers' perception of you. As a result of the actions of salespeople who have come before you, many of your customers will walk into your business *expecting* not to be able to trust you. There are concepts throughout this book that can guide you through that, but exhibiting legendary follow-through will accelerate that process. This alone will increase your chances of closing the deal with your customers.

In addition, I can tell you firsthand that mastering follow-through will also increase your confidence, as you will face challenges that I will discuss more in Chapter 12, where you will need confidence to overcome the typical obstacles salespeople face daily.

One way to drive home your message of legendary commitment to follow through is in the manner in which you implement it. As I said earlier, the best way to do so is to react immediately with an answer or by providing someone who can do so. Sometimes, it's just not possible to answer on the spot because no one else is available, and you must commit to follow through on it later.

Another important element of legendary follow-through is the level of detail in your commitment. It must include what you will do, when you will do it, and how you will do it, along with acceptance of approval of your customer. A typical example of how you would say that might be, "I will research your question on how the suspension system is constructed on the Tiffen 32HW motor home and get back to you by Wednesday, April 3rd, at 3:00 p.m. Would you prefer that I call you or email you with my response?"

Once the customer agrees, you are solidly committed to act within the time frame you agreed to. Any violation of that comes with a huge credibility risk and will likely eliminate the chance of you getting a deal even if you're five minutes late.

Sometimes, circumstances beyond your control make it impossible for you to honor that commitment exactly as stated. When that happens, you MUST contact the customer on the exact day and time you committed to and communicate that information to him/her. The next step will be to make a new commitment (with a shorter time frame) on what you will do and when you will do it again with an exact day and time.

I cannot emphasize enough the importance of making specific commitments and honoring them exactly as agreed. Each time you do what you said you would, when you said you would do it that further cements your word, your bond, and your credibility with your customer. Missing the commitment even once can, and likely will, ruin the credibility of your word because it will create doubt in your customer's mind. Let's face it, whether it's right or not, or fair or not, customers are "What have you done for me lately" people-- and they have short memories.

Once again, enacting all this is a DECISION. It's one that the top 10% of salespeople have made long ago, and one that separates them from you. If you want to be in the top 10% of the sales staff at your business, this is the first step you need to take. This isn't a temporary fix; it's a lifetime decision. In doing so, you will find that it also carries over to your personal life. How people judge each other in customer and salesperson relationships is quite similar to how it plays out in personal relationships and friendships.

When I was selling RVs, I had multiple customers tell me they purchased from me because I had excellent follow-through.

Going forward with legendary follow-through begins with your belief that it **can** make a significance in your success, so let's start now. Make the ironclad commitment that you need today, and ten years from now, not only will you be very proud you did, but I'll bet you'll be making a boatload more money, as well.

12

Overcoming Obstacles

Up to this point in the book, I have reviewed all the ways that a salesperson can build on the skills and techniques to form comfort, rapport, and trust with the customer and then use that as the foundation for a successful closing and a commitment to buy.

Even when all that goes as planned, there are a few additional obstacles that most salespeople must overcome to achieve success. Some of those are addressed in the training they receive when they are initially hired, but many are not.

There are three main obstacles that salespeople must not only be aware of, but also actively implement steps (often on their own) to handle when they arise. My experience in hiring, training, and coaching salespeople has shown me that steps can be taken to minimize them or prevent them from happening in the first place.

Many new salespeople have either been let go or have left the sales business on their own because they failed to address these obstacles, and some were right on the verge of success. Even with solid company training, it seems to take many salespeople a year or two to obtain the knowledge they need and feel comfortable (and confident) with both 1) adequate product and 2) how to navigate all the different kinds of customers with whom they might work.

Although there are many things salespeople have to contend with in those first few years, there are four that stand out as having the biggest impact on salespeople trying to learn to navigate their customers:

1. Overcoming the negative perception of salespeople.
2. The fear of customer rejection.
3. The fear of failure.
4. Managing a commission income.

Overcoming the Negative Perception of Salespeople

As stated earlier in this book, most of us have dealt with a poor salesperson at some point in our lives, and the memory of that does tend to hang with us for quite a while, at least until we work with a good one who restores our faith.

Years ago when I first started selling RVs in a medium-sized city in upstate New York, the very first customer I ever worked with was a fairly easy and enjoyable experience. It took about two hours, and it resulted in me selling an RV at a good gross profit and commission. I thought, *Wow, I'm going to love this.*

However, the second customer (Joseph) I worked with HATED salespeople, was mouthy, and frankly, verbally abusive. When I introduced myself to him at the front door, the very first thing he said to me was (please excuse my *French*): *"Just so you know, I HATE salespeople--you're all assholes, and all you want to do is screw customers so you can make a good commission at my expense. So don't try any of that crap with me, or I am walking out!"*

Sadly, customers can be brutal at times. I was new and didn't expect that, so of course, it caught me off guard, and I wobbled a bit. Once I regained my senses, I decided to ask him what happened, so I wouldn't make the same mistake. It was a long story, but I shut up and listened to every word for as long as it took. Why? Because he was telling me what not to do with him.

Once he blew off a lot of steam, I decided to let him take as long as HE needed to get everything off his chest, calm down, and start to relax. I didn't speak for quite a while and continued to listen closely. I was new, so I took my cues from him and didn't try to move forward until he indicated he was ready. Once the emotions calmed down, I decided to move one step at a time, letting him know what I wanted to do at each step and asking his permission if that was ok with him. He liked that, and we got along fine. We spent a few hours together, and he didn't buy anything but was happy with how I handled him.

A few days later, someone (whom I didn't know) called and made an appointment to work with me. I was surprised because I had not built a customer base yet. When he showed up, he said that his friend, Joseph, referred him to me because he felt respected for the first time while working with a salesperson.

This customer didn't buy anything either, but the experience of it all was worth more than any commission, as it taught me a great deal about the value of the first impression, even with someone who hated salespeople. This formed the foundation for the first ten to fifteen minutes of every customer I worked with going forward.

Over the years, I became hyper-focused on listening more than talking and being observant in the first few minutes when working with customers. I learned that many of them had awful perceptions of salespeople from their experiences with some of our competitors and walked in with a negative attitude about working with one.

The general attitude was that salespeople are

- Pushy and aggressive.
- Lack authenticity and honesty.
- Are sleezy and manipulative.

- Over promise and underdeliver.
- Withhold information about what they're selling.
- Are "bullshitters."

I have sprinkled suggestions throughout this book up to this point on how to handle customers in the first few minutes. Below is a recap (and checklist) of things all salespeople must do in those critical first few minutes to lighten the emotional load for your customers shortly after greeting them. I suggest checking off the ones you need to work on or focus on going forward.

- Forget what happened with your last customer, whether good or bad, and start with a *blank sheet of paper*. I like to call it *emptying your head*.

- SLOW DOWN in those critical first few minutes. Let those first few moments breathe a bit before jumping into your selling system.

- Read your customer's body language to establish a pace that THEY are comfortable with (not you).

- Listen more than talk to allow your customer the time and space to get comfortable speaking.

- Make comfort, rapport, and trust building a higher priority than jumping in front of your product too soon.

- **Ask your customer** how you can best help him/her and work with him/her today. The customer will tell you exactly what to do, and then you need to go do that.

- Don't know your product, so MASTER IT, and master your competitors' products as well. Why? Because your customer expects that.

- Don't *show up and throw up* all the information you have about your product. Develop a collaborative product presentation that involves your customer and his/her needs and wants every step of the way.

- Prevent objections from happening, as outlined in Chapter 9. Don't be on pins and needles waiting for their objections to get the best of you.

- Don't compromise honesty – ever – even if it's uncomfortable for two minutes.

Fear of Failure

Every occupation has some fear of failure, but a position as a salesperson is near the top of that list. A good salesperson sells to approximately 30% of his/her customers, meaning that 70% of them won't buy from the salesperson. However, those numbers represent only the top salespeople in each business. There are another 50% or so who move in and out of good months and bad months (depending on the time of year), which leaves about 30% of the sales staff who frankly considers looking for work elsewhere because being in sales just isn't a good fit for them (Morin).

It's normal to feel pressure from sales managers to hit monthly sales goals and a constant reminder when you're in the middle of a bad month. When this happens, it's human nature for emotions to fester, constantly wondering when the next customer who walks in the front door will be willing to buy something.

With so many people looking for work now, the leash tends to be shorter on non-performance when it happens. It's human nature that when you combine a salesperson having a bad month with pressure from the sales manager and your spouse because you're not bringing a check home, the stress is going to build up. As a result, it becomes difficult to handle that pressure in a way that doesn't become obvious to the customer standing in front of you. Let's face it; we're all human.

Fear of failure is an obstacle every salesperson should be made aware of before entering the sales field. When I was interviewing candidates for sales positions, I asked at least ten questions to try to establish how a person would handle those off months because they are bound to happen in any sales business.

Salespeople can only manage what they can control. Becoming an expert on their product and using the concepts and ideas in this book can help anyone get out of a slump if the person is committed to following the steps in it.

Much of this can be minimized with a strong work ethic, an ongoing desire to learn, and a maturity about the potential ups and downs of selling. Not getting too high in great months or too low in rough months is a great way to start. Somehow, the sun does come up tomorrow, and staying positive and controlling what you can control is a good recipe for success.

Fear of Rejection

No one likes to be rejected in any aspect of life--not at work, at home, or with friends. Too few businesses take steps in the interview process to ensure that they are hiring people who have the maturity and confidence to handle rejection, so eventually, they succumb to the pressures of it. Some companies just aren't honest about the reality of this in their interviews, as they don't want to scare applicants away from working there.

Of all the things that can derail someone trying to develop and grow a career in sales, handling the fear of rejection may be the single biggest obstacle he/she faces. I have seen more salespeople leave the business because rejection has completely worn them emotionally after a year or two.

Salespeople, even the great ones, will hear the word *"No"* more often than the word *"Yes"* in selling. Following many of the steps in this book can help reduce the chance of rejection, but sometimes even the best efforts of a really good salesperson aren't going to be enough.
Having a positive outlook, understanding that when customers say *"No,"* they often mean not right now is a good approach. Every customer buys differently from the last and not taking it personally when a customer chooses not to buy something is critical.

A missed opportunity salespeople do quite often is they continue to repeat the same mistake over and over because they didn't take the time to replay the customer experience and analyze pluses and minuses after the customer leaves.

After EVERY customer visit, salespeople MUST take a few minutes and replay every step of what just occurred in a customer interaction, whether they purchased or not. Starting at the first few moments of the "meet & greet" and replaying every step as it happened will help a salesperson identify where he/she might have lost a customer's interest, whether it is in rapport building or the product demonstration. Identifying at what point rapport and trust were earned (or not) will offer valuable information on what to do next.

Each of these *moments of truth*, as I call them, is instrumental in mastering each step in the sales process, ESPECIALLY in the first fifteen minutes of meeting the customer. More sales are lost during this period than any other, but too many salespeople don't pay attention to it.

If salespeople take the approach that LITTLE THINGS MATTER and proceed through the interaction with a customer, they will become skilled at catching mistakes before they happen the next time.

I asked my resource group for their thoughts on their fear of rejection and how they handle rejection, and here are some of their thoughts and suggestions.

Brian Osborn (real estate agent) very honestly says, "This is a tough one, and I am one needing coaching on this because I truly approach my business on a personal level so that the rejection can feel more personal." *Many salespeople might claim that rejection doesn't bother them, but if they were honest, like Brian, they would admit that rejection does sting, even if it's only for a minute or two. It's important to acknowledge it and move on.*

Adam Isabella (insurance broker) says, "It doesn't hurt to take another shot if you don't get the sale the first time."

Ryan Meca (V.P. and financial advisor, Merrill Lynch) says, "Understand that it's going to happen. No one has a 100% success rate, so don't feel like you're a failure if a client says no to you."

Diane Luksis (health coach) says, "Develop a shift in your mindset. Don't look at it as being rejected. Customers may come back when they're ready."

Erik Betz, training & development specialist, says, "Remember, not every customer will be a perfect fit, but that's ok. Each 'No' is a step closer to a 'Yes.'"

Everyone in sales needs to have quiet confidence to move on when a customer rejects his/her attempts to close the sale. It's an everyday component of selling that comes with the job, and having reasonable expectations about it, along with maturity in handling it, is also a mandatory part of accepting a sales position, especially if you want to stay in it long term.

Managing a Commission-based Income

This is a topic I hardly ever see written about. For a salesperson who has transitioned from a job with a weekly or bi-weekly paycheck, I have seen significant struggles with salespeople adjusting to managing their money and paying their monthly bills.

It is one thing to depend on receiving a paycheck every week regardless of performance, but to get a job in sales and receive a different amount in your check every week that is based on individual sales results, well, that's a whole different can of worms.

In most companies, selling is a performance-based business, and the paycheck received is based on commissions earned. Every company does things a bit differently, but in many companies, if you don't sell, you'll have a small (or no) paycheck, which would be tough for anyone to pay living expenses. That is stressful. Can you imagine walking in the front door of your home and telling your spouse that there's no paycheck this week? It's not a fun conversation to have.

Many commission-based businesses have some seasonality to them. No matter where it is in the country, the weather can affect when people buy and how much they're willing to spend, which means there are on seasons and off seasons. Holiday seasons tend to have a significant effect on most commission businesses, as well. Do you see a lot of people buying cars or RVs during Christmas? I sure don't.

Human nature is a funny thing and so is the responsibility to manage money. I can't tell you how many situations I have seen where a salesperson will have a great month, only to be followed by an awful month. So often there is the temptation that after having a record month, some salespeople feel they have earned the right to relax and take their foot off the pedal the following month. I have seen it happen over and over--a huge mistake. The downside here, other than the obvious one, is that there will be no paycheck the following month.

Whether created by seasonality, advertising, or availability of product, salespeople must strike when the iron is hot, put the pedal to the floor, and make the money when business is right in front of their noses. Once the seasons change, things can easily go dark again, and everybody is stressed.

During peak seasons, salespeople must restrict how much they spend on disposable income. They need to take only what they need and think long-term, not just short-term, and plan to cover the lean months they know will be coming.

Economic conditions and interest rates can strongly dictate market activity in sales businesses, as well. If interest rates are high (or unstable), people are simply unwilling to make purchases that are financed. There's just too much economic uncertainty to take that risk. If that happens in the middle of a peak season, which in many industries is happening at the time of this writing, there IS NO peak season to build up your bank at work or home to get you through the upcoming projected down season. That puts many salespeople one step from bankruptcy. Again, that's stress.

The big takeaway in accepting a commission sales position at any time is to go in lean with the weekly draw (paycheck), set a goal of what will be needed in the bank for reserve, and stick to it. The salespeople who choose not to develop a plan similar to this are often the
ones who leave their commission sales positions in the first year or two. They simply can't make the transition from the safety and security of a weekly paycheck to a commission check.

Don't let this happen to you. Once the tail starts wagging the dog and the finances start to fall apart, all the potential benefits of a performance-based sales job are washed away.

Start NOW—make a plan to control your variable income before it controls YOU.

13

Referrals Based on Trust

Interviewing, hiring, training, observing, and coaching salespeople over the years has convinced me that the majority are good, hard-working people trying to build a successful career and an income they can depend on to support their family. Most work hard to do the right thing every day and try to overcome some of the perceptions customers might have of them. Sounds great, right? Why then do so many leave thousands of dollars on the table by not making any effort with the referral side of the business? Honestly, it blows my mind.

A great deal of statistics have been done by multiple organizations reflecting the feeble effort salespeople make in pursuing referrals. One was by Dale Carnegie, where they found that only 11%--**yes 11%**--of salespeople took the initiative to ask their customers for a referral. They asked customers if they would be willing to give a reference, with 91% saying "*Yes*," they would be willing to do so if they were asked to do so (https://dalecarnegie.com).

Nielsen also did a survey and found out that 92% of the customers they spoke to would trust a referral given to them by someone they know (https://nielsen.com).

A survey reported by Market Force found that 84% of customers' online purchases are highly influenced by their friends and social media posts

(ANAmarketers.)

What is the conclusion here? People not only want their friends to tell them about the positive experiences they have when purchasing something, but they also want to tell others about theirs as well! If you think about when we work with a salesperson and truly enjoy the experience, what do we want to do next? We want to tell everyone about it!

Many of us want to go on social media and announce our new car or RV to the world with pictures or videos. Spend just ten minutes on any social media site, and you will see verification of this. Brevet did a survey and found that 78% of salespeople use social media to advertise and outperform their peers, but for some, there is business out there that they are not actively pursuing. As a result, roughly 70% of the customers walk out the door without ever buying anything at all (Williams).

There are other reasons why EVERY salesperson should make asking for referrals a huge priority in his/her day. I have seen over and over that the referral customer is an easier sale because he/she received the referral to work with a salesperson from a trusted friend. This reduces a great deal of the anxiety a customer might normally feel walking into a business and allows both the customer and the salesperson to get down to business much quicker.

A referral customer also tends to be a higher profit sale. The reduced tension and increased trust established by a referral from a friend also helps the customer relax and be more open to being upsold on add-ons that increase the gross profit (and commission) in the deal.

As I have stated emphatically throughout this book, the word of emphasis here is **TRUST**. Trust is the straw that stirs the drink with customers. The referral customer already has some level of comfort, which leads to rapport, which results in trust and much more quickly than a customer who hasn't enjoyed the benefit of a referral from a friend.

Another key component that can help lay the groundwork to ask for a referral is providing exceptional customer service. Listening to a customer's needs and understanding exactly what is wanted and why he/she wants it is something most customers will pay great attention to and can lead to a referral after the sale. The component that takes this to another level is the legendary follow-through that was discussed in Chapter 11. Once the customer perceives that a salesperson has heard what he/she wants and why it is wanted, the expectation for exceptional follow-through goes up substantially. The salesperson who delivers with solid follow-through ends up with another arrow in his/her quiver when it comes to the right to ask for a referral.

To recap, building trust, listening to a customer's needs, and responding to that with the right product that's in his/her budget, following up by doing what you said you would do when you said you would do it, and providing exceptional customer service will set the stage for a referral. You would be surprised how many customers are disappointed that you didn't ask for a referral when everything above was achieved. Why? Because they WANT to tell others about it. It's human nature. So, when is the right time to ask for a referral? Great question.

My experience has taught me that when the deal is at its peak of emotions, typically on the day when the customer picks up his/her new furniture, car, RV, or whatever they purchased is the best time to ask for a referral. Some salespeople wait for a week or so and follow up with a phone call to be sure everything has gone as planned, and then the salesperson asks for the referral, but my experience has been that doing so on pick up or delivery day is best.

Even though some salespeople recognize the moment when their customers are the happiest, they don't have the **confidence** to ask for a referral. One thing that affects a salesperson's confidence more than anything else is not making money, which often lands him/her at the bottom of the sales board hanging on the wall in the sales manager's office. When I first started learning to sell, I was hesitant to ask customers for a referral, even when I knew they were satisfied with how I had worked with them.

What changed all that? One customer was so happy with how the process went with me, they talked to five friends that evening, and the next day, I received phone calls from all five to set appointments. That led to selling to four of the five and earning me salesperson of the month in only my third month of selling. From that day on, I asked **every customer I sold to** for not just one referral, but MULTIPLE referrals—and I followed up on everyone going forward. I was a believer every day after that.

My commitment to asking for referrals resulted in multiple benefits that helped me become a top salesperson in the company. When a customer refers someone else and the referral purchases from you, it increases his/her loyalty to you. They become an advocate for you and will tell everyone about you. This results in a higher closing ratio over time because you are being given higher-quality leads by customers who purchased from you. This situation helped me absolutely fall in love with the term word of mouth marketing because of the snowball effect of it all.

Of course, the way in which you ask for referrals matters as well. Some salespeople have a standard line they use, but others craft it to be consistent with how they have spoken to their customers throughout the selling process.

Diane Luksis, metabolic health coach, says, "You need to ask at the right time, right after your customer has a big win."
Also, she likes to add something of value as a thank you for the referral, saying, "As a thank you for your testimonial or personal referral, I would like to offer you a free coaching session with me."

Ryan Meca, vice president with Merrill Lynch, adds, "If my clients don't feel comfortable saying something like, 'You have to talk to Ryan,' then I need to deepen our relationship before asking for a referral. The biggest benefit from this was that I no longer lived off the up desk because I often scheduled multiple daily appointments, typically on slower days, so I could be available on the floor for the busy days. It's a win-win proposition that can happen to you as well!"

Here's another reason why referrals work. When customers give referrals, most don't take that lightly. Their word and personal reputation are at stake, so they take that responsibility very seriously. On top of all that, because they support you and are loyal customers, they don't want to let you down. Interestingly enough one of my customers (who helped me with multiple referrals) eventually came to work for us because he fell in love with the concept of selling.

In closing, too many salespeople overthink how to ask for a referral. Of course, everyone is unique in how he/she prefers to do so, but the key is **not to overthink it**. Just be yourself, ask it in a way that's consistent with how you typically speak, and don't drag it out. Get to the point. Something as simple as saying, "If you are as happy in working with me as you seem to be, would you be comfortable asking some of your friends if they might like to work with me as well?"

The simplest and most honest way to convince you to get on board with the gold mine of referrals is to ask this: "Do you want an easy way that is right in front of your nose to make more money?" Then jump on the bandwagon of referrals today—not tonight, not tomorrow—TODAY.

You will be proud of yourself as will your spouse and banker. Challenge yourself to not let a customer leave before asking for a referral. Even if a customer doesn't buy something from you, most are more than willing to help pass along a referral about a positive experience.

14

Managing Self-Development

When I recall the salespeople I have hired, trained, coached, supervised, or have known over the years, one of the most frustrating observations I have made is the high percentage who fail to take ownership of their own self-development.

Of course, the companies that employ them have the responsibility to train all new salespeople on their products, selling systems, company philosophy, policies, procedures, and paperwork. They also must retrain existing salespeople to keep them sharp and up to date on changes in all those areas. Unfortunately, the average company spends $10,000-15,000 hiring a new salesperson but only $2,000 on the initial sales training (Morin).

Some companies have a formal sales trainer position, but many do not. Far too often, the training for a new salesperson is assigned to another salesperson on the staff to train someone who will compete with him/her for the next customer who walks in. It's a cost-saving move, but does that really work? When I was selling, I was quickly named to train all new salespeople, which I did with hard work and solid intentions to help them as best I could, but does that really sound like a good idea?

As a result, most new salespeople tend to perceive that the responsibility for their initial training and development lies with the company that just hired them. Sounds fair, right? Too many companies shove the new person on the floor to sell and say, "Good luck." That's one reason why most newly hired salespeople last about a year and a half and then leave.

In addition, have you seen any company train its sales staff on how to perform an effective "meet & greet" with a customer or to achieve comfort, rapport, and trust with a customer? I have not. Too many rely solely on the sparkling personality of their salespeople to successfully handle that critical step. Or how about identifying and taking steps to address the often-hidden anxiety with which their customers walk in with and then what to do about it?

I am not aware of any company that trains sales staff on how to handle difficult situations with customers (mentioned in an earlier chapter in this book), not only to prevent objections, but how to *handle* them when they occur. And if customer history has taught us anything, they WILL happen.

To give credit where credit is due, most companies do a decent job of basic training, especially for new salespeople, but it seems to end there. Those in seasonal businesses do tend to train more in the off season, but what do they do during the season to stay sharp? For some, they don't do much.

The current economic conditions have forced companies to reduce budgets in many areas, either by eliminating the trainer position or cutting back on the money budgeted for in-house training sessions. So where does that leave most salespeople? They need to pick up the slack and take much more ownership in the following areas.

Managing Self-Development

As I observe the best of the best, the cream of the crop, the top 10-20% of salespeople who consistently deliver strong performance and the commission to go with it, one thing this group does is to do the work of keeping themselves sharp and not relying on the company to do it for them. This group perceives the company-sponsored training as a starting point, and no more. They accept and fully own the responsibility of **being their own HR Manager**, which they implement in all twelve months of the year and not just in seasonal down periods.

The first steps in managing self-development are acceptance and buy-in. It's deciding that the chief responsibility for becoming sharp and staying sharp rests with the person in the mirror--YOU. It's a commitment to own the responsibility for what you do, how you do it, and how you manage your downtime at work every day from now on. This is not something that can be accomplished with a casual attitude. It's a serious step that sets the stage for owning your development from now on.

This all begins with a micro-breakdown of every aspect of the customer experience that's over and above what the company teaches with a laser-like, step-by-step focus, starting with how to approach a new customer upon making eye contact with him/her.

As I have said throughout this book, those early minutes are often when deals are lost (and most salespeople don't realize it). That is typically followed by hours of conversation, product presentations, addressing objections, attempts at closing, and finally, the customer walking out, saying, "I want to go home and think about it."

When I first started selling many years ago, I worked with someone who had been there for many years and earned the salesperson of the year award for twelve years in a row. I wondered just how he was able to do that, but just a few observations gave me the answer. His ONLY priority in the early stages of meeting his customer was to build a solid rapport. **Everything else has to wait.** I would walk by his office, where he would be sitting at his desk, having very casual conversations with his arms folded. There were times when I would walk by fifteen, thirty, and even forty-five minutes later, and he was still in the same position. No progress or so it seemed.

What was he doing? He was allowing his customer to relieve his/her anxiety, relax, feel comfortable, and start to trust him **before ever going to step one in the sales process, no matter how long it took.** He would ask a question and listen, then ask another question and listen over and over and over. I would watch the anxious look on his customer's face slowly slip away to be replaced with smiles and, eventually, comfort and laughter. In time, they were *yucking it up* to the point where the customer was just having fun and even forgot why he/she walked in to begin with.

It was only THEN that the sales process could begin.

For some crazy reason, companies just don't teach this. It's about achieving normal human feelings we all need to be comfortable with **before** allowing a salesperson to take us through a shopping process. Salespeople need to realize that this is the first step in managing their own self-development. Review those initial stages of a customer experience, break them down word-for-word if necessary, and identify the small mistakes that take a sales process off track. This can only happen if salespeople slow things down and really consider those important early minutes with a new customer.

This is a step that my friend, sales trainer Jack Daly, calls a **high-payoff activity**. It's the first step salespeople must take in their downtime to start rebuilding human relations skills with customers. It's also the first step in managing **your own** self-development. Why? No one else will do this for you.

When I was selling many years ago, I used this as a starting point to develop my own personal sales playbook. In this playbook, I captured every element and every small detail I needed to implement, to ensure that the little (but critical) moments like the one mentioned in this chapter were identified and followed up on with every customer. When I became the director of employee development for my company, I expanded this concept into a sales playbook for all salespeople, helping each one improve trust-building and turn us into top performers year after year, resulting in consecutive sales records for our company.

I expanded the **High Payoff Activities** portion of the playbook to include everything salespeople should focus on when business is slow. The idea was to use every available minute sharpening the saw to help them be more prepared when the next customer walked in. It's not just about a commitment to self-development; it's about having a clear purpose and understanding of how we would spend each available minute of downtime working to get better instead of sitting in each other's office talking about a game we watched last night or what fun activities we did over the weekend.

I identified a series of tangible activities we would work on and check off, one by one, until we mastered each one. The result was that there weren't any situations we couldn't handle, no matter when they arose in the sales process with a customer. We also practiced these in weekly meetings and role plays to hone our skills even further.

The following is a quick reference guide to use as a **starting point** to get you thinking about your own individual high-payoff activities and to begin this self-development process.

HIGH PAYOFF ACTIVITIES
(Starting Point for You to Build On)

Sales Planning & Results
- Set annual and monthly goals on Units, Gross Sales, Average Sales, Appointments
- Identify specific activities that can drive each
- Review all results weekly and monthly
- Strategize general customer approaches with the sales manager
- Identify one major downtime plan at the beginning of each workday

Product Knowledge
- Attain superior knowledge of every product, using brochures, videos, manufacturer representative walkthroughs, and/or videos
- Identify at least five talking points for each product feature
- Develop a list of each product feature and identify the need or problem each addresses
- Develop and role practice collaborative demonstrations to apply product features to customer needs
- Practice adjustments in pace, word selection, and talking points regarding every product feature
- Spend fifteen minutes each day working on developing your own personal sales playbook
- Develop and type a list of "why buy now" that can be handed out to customers before closing attempts
- Develop ten different closing lines to be used with customers
- Develop situational responses to the statement, "I want to go home and think about it"

Appointments
- Set appointment goals monthly and weekly

- Make confirming calls or text messages for every appointment
- Develop opening lines and statements when making calls to set up appointments
- Prepare appointment packets in advance (to be handed out to customers upon arrival):
    - Updated product news
    - New product features just out
    - Sale promotions on individual products
    - Bio sheet for yourself
    - Written customer testimonials received

Personal Branding
- Post on social media according to company procedures and guidelines
- Participate in three personal networking opportunities weekly

Organization & Planning
- Pre-plan and prioritize next-day follow-through and opportunities at the end of each day
- Make the completion of the daily follow-through list the highest priority

Customer Follow-Through
- Set goals for daily customer follow-through calls and contacts
- Develop individual customer strategies and approaches with the sales manager
- Text or email a thank you to every customer before he/she leaves the parking lot
- Write and mail a handwritten thank-you card after every customer appointment
- Write a lead-development plan for the next day.

Each personal sales playbook must be developed and crafted to reflect personal priorities and activities to impact individual performance and results, which can be different for everyone. The ideas above are suggestions as a starting point. The key will be to take action and take the first steps today to develop your own and then begin following up immediately.

Another possible challenge all salespeople face is being able to exercise their right to say "*No*" to a customer. Even though many think they do, most customers aren't truly aware of the product that best fits them, regardless of what products they saw others purchasing.

It would be wise to make a list of possible situations each salesperson may face, where they may have to push back against a customer and say "*No*" to him/her. What's important is not what is said but HOW it is said. Customers expect salespeople not to allow them to go down the wrong path and buy the wrong thing because ultimately, the salesperson would be blamed for that. Adding a list of situations where a salesperson might have to say "*No*" to a customer will be helpful. Referring to the examples listed earlier in this book can be a starting point for that.

Let's face it; at times, all salespeople can be lazy. I will not be popular in saying that, but observations over the years have proven that to me. The sales manager shouldn't be the only person motivating individual accountability for follow-through on this chapter. It must come from within you and be driven by you. In many cases, this fact, alone, is what separates top salespeople from those in the middle of the pack.

Top salespeople simply cannot accept less and use every minute of downtime to assess, analyze what they can do better, and then take steps to implement that. There is no sitting in their offices playing games on the computer or watching a baseball game when there are no customers.

Of course, you have the right to decide not to develop your own sales playbook, but I can assure you that the top 10-20% will take advantage of this and will make more money as a result.

From this point forward, I would like to see you use this chapter to challenge yourself to be fully accountable for what you do or don't do in your own downtime at work. Start right now; you will be better prepared to build a customer shopping experience that results in greater sales.

Another direct benefit of taking charge of your downtime minutes to hone your skills will be a higher individual level of confidence, something every salesperson will need to rely on when dealing with stressful situations with customers. Customers do tend to notice a salesperson's level of confidence, and frankly, they expect it. Having an inner level of confidence can help diffuse potential objections and push customers struggling to decide to buy from you over the fence and to say "Yes."

In addition, some customers like to make a game out of working with a salesperson. It's a mini competition to see who will win. Some of the toughest customers I have ever had turned out to be a referral machine for me because I had the confidence to stand up to them. Even the tough ones respect a salesperson who has his/her act together and has the confidence to engage in a little back and forth. Some will test your will just to see how far they can take you and will back down when you prove that you have both confidence and an attention to detail—tactfully, of course.

Let go! Start now to be your OWN HR Manager—take control of what you do every day and how you do it—every small detail and be laser-focused.

Your sales manager and your bank account will thank you for it.

15

"I Want to Go Home and Think About It"

One of the most commonly used objections salespeople must deal with often after spending two, three, or four hours of exhaustive work demonstrating a product to a customer is for them to derail the process with a phrase like, "I want to go home and think about it."

When that happens, it's typical that the salesperson is caught off guard, thinking, *Everything has gone so well. The customer seems to love the product and loves the price, supported by positive comments throughout the process. The air seems to be let out of the entire effort that just took place.*

Why then does this objection happen?

The first question you need to consider is simple: Is that *really* an objection?

Most of the salespeople I have hired, coached, and trained would swear that it is. However, even though it looks, sounds, and feels like one, I contend that although there is a chance that it might be, it's more likely that it's a **stall** than an objection. For those times when it appears to be an honest objection, 99% of the time, it's self-inflicted by the salesperson because of a step or steps that were omitted earlier in the visit. More often than not, salespeople set up the perfect opportunity for a customer to use that excuse by missing things that should have been done earlier in the process. One of the reasons I write books on sales and coach salespeople is to help them close those gaps.

All too often, the first mistake salespeople make is to *blame the customer* instead of looking in the mirror.

I have heard all the excuses over the years: The customer didn't really want to buy in the first place; they were trying to find something to do for three hours; they were looking for ideas to use at home; and, on and on. When a salesperson points at a customer, he/she needs to remember that three fingers on the same hand are pointing back at him/her and for good reason.

So, what are some of the things that could have left the door open for a customer to drop that bomb right when the salesperson was going in for the close? Here are just a few of the first places salespeople should look to prevent this situation from happening in the future.

Not Achieving Comfort, Rapport, and Trust

My observations of salespeople during the first fifteen minutes of a customer "meet & greet" reveal that they rush through this initial period, where the customer needs to be allowed to breathe, relax, and feel comfortable that the salesperson can be trusted, as discussed in earlier chapters. Rushing through that critical period is not negotiable, and the salesperson will pay the price later if he/she bypasses that opportunity. No matter what, WINNING THE CUSTOMER should be the priority, and no salesperson should go on to step two until that happens, no matter how long it takes (and some may take a while).

Rushing the Customer in Front of Their Product

Hurrying a customer in front of the product is a shortcut way for a salesperson to avoid the hard work of building trust, and implements a controlled step-by-step process that allows the customer to catch his/her breath in those first few minutes. Salespeople need to let their customers' excitement relax, so they can feel comfortable communicating everything the salesperson needs to know to put them in front of a product that is perfect for them. Not just the product that has all the bells and whistles the company likes to brag about, but the one that fills a need or solves a problem for the customer.

Not Identifying the Customer's "Stretch" Budget

All customers have a budget, whether they're willing to tell the salesperson about it or not. Many salespeople do a decent job of finding out the *preferred* amount of money the customers would like to spend. Most stop right there. That is a mistake. Salespeople need to push that one step further and ask the customer what amount he/she *would be willing to spend* for a product that meets all the requirements and more.

Although they might not say it at first, many customers have an extra amount of budget they're willing to pay for the product that exceeds their expectations. Instead of being up front with a higher budget range, some salespeople try to **trap** customers into spending more money by getting them to fall in love with something that's over their budget. This often doesn't work and is a major fear that most customers have about salespeople. Getting a soft commitment earlier in the conversation before looking at the product is far less intimidating to them and can be used to bump them in price later because they agreed to it earlier.

Identifying a Customer's Problem to Solve or a Need to Fill

Too many salespeople try to give an all-world product presentation by listing all of the goodies that a product offers, rather than finding out specifically what needs customers have to fill or problems to solve and building their product presentation **around that**. Once a product presentation solves the wants and needs, the other cool features on the product can be used to take them up on the offer to go a little more in budget than they mentioned earlier.

Establishing How a Customer Prefers the Salesperson to Work with Him/Her

Not all salespeople are compatible with their customers because we all have different ways in which we like to speak, conduct ourselves, and demonstrate products.

The best way to know exactly how customers would prefer us to work with them is to *ask them*. If it's not obvious as to the way your customer prefers you to work with or present a product to him/her, ask directly: "For me to work with you in a way that's most comfortable for you, how would you prefer that we proceed from here?" "Is there any specific manner in which you would like me to present the product to you or tell you about it?" Most customers will tell you exactly what they want you to do and how to do it. All you need to do is make that one quick adjustment, and your chance of building rapport and trust can rise quickly.

Not Right Now

Finally, when customers say they want to go home and think about it, MOST OF THE TIME they don't mean "*No.*" They mean "not right now." The key is when they say that, relax and do not take it personally or show any emotion, but you do need to investigate further as to what it is that's holding them back and whether it's logical or emotional.

Here are some approaches I have effectively used, depending on the situation and your comfort level, but each works, depending on the situation.

"OK, so I understand that you would like to go home and think about it. That's all good with me, but to help me prepare to follow up with you in a week or so, what is it that you'll need to go home and think about?"

"Other than price, what is it you'll need to go home and think about?"

"It seems like there is something preventing you from moving forward. Would you care to share?"

"I completely understand. You want to think about it, but on a scale of 1-10, where would you say you stand at this moment?" This should be followed up with, "What would make it a 10 right now?"

If there is a real objection, using one of these follow-up questions can help to reveal it, and then steps can be taken to address that accordingly. However, don't be surprised that many (if not most) customers won't have an answer to either question. It's just a way to buy time and avoid having to decide to buy on the spot. When that happens, it's very important to set an appointment immediately for no more than twenty-four to forty-eight hours to get them back in to see you.

For some customers, buying on the spot just doesn't feel right, but coming back in after a few days will lessen the pressure they're feeling at that moment.

As we stated earlier in this book, most buying decisions are emotional rather than logical, but reading the body language cues that accompany customers' responses can help to narrow down the thing(s) making them uncomfortable and preventing them from saying "Yes" to buying.

However, there is one exception to this, and that's the analytical customer–the thinker. This is the one customer who MUST go home and think about it. This is the customer who will go home and pore over the data or information you handed out during the product presentation and will READ EVERY WORD. Why? Because that's how this person processes decision making. He/She has to do it this way. For this customer, you will need to give him/her time to think, review what you said, read what you handed out, AND verify it all with the internet or other research.

For this customer, this delay tactic isn't about trusting or not trusting you; it's about HIM/HER. It's normal to process information and the resulting decisions in this manner, so you will need to give this person time and space to do so. However, before leaving, you must reach a mutually agreed-upon day and time for you to follow up, and he/she will honor that because this customer prefers to work with an end goal in mind.

This is the one customer that, if you push too hard at this point, you will push him/her away. However, if the quality of the information you presented complements what handouts you gave the customer when assessing it on his/her own, you will have developed trust with the customer, and he/she will eventually buy from you.

Another thing I will say about this fact-based customer is he/she can be very loyal and can bring you many referrals. Because he/she is perceived to be knowledgeable and information-based, people tend to listen to this person when referring a salesperson. As a result, this is a customer with whom it is worth being patient.

One more thing—for this customer, it's also advisable to avoid too much social conversation in your closing due to his/her business-like, *just the facts, please* approach. I have worked with quite a few of these customers. They are just not into small talk.

Regardless of the circumstances that led up to them saying they want to go home and think about it, it's essential to stay calm and take a one-step-at-a-time approach, being confident that the sale will happen. It may not happen on that day, but with good communications, understanding, and follow-through, you will have a good chance of a return visit and a "Yes" to buying from you.

16

A Call to Action

Well, you've read the previous 15 Chapters, and that has led you to this **moment of truth**.

Why do I call this a *moment of truth*? Because it's one thing to read about ideas to help you make more money. It's another thing to decide to take action to implement those.

Now that you have been given detailed guidance on how to be more productive in your downtime, turn the trust you have built with your customer into potentially earning more money. You're now at the point where you need to decide how to implement it directly into your daily activities.

I've reviewed that listening to your customers and setting a pace that's comfortable for them helps calm their anxiety and make it easier for them to pay attention to what you're saying. Also, nailing the greeting, adjusting your presentation to a way that THEY prefer, and mastering legendary follow-through are just a few of the key building blocks of trust the customer MUST recognize to achieve the comfort and trust to eventually buy something from you.

I have shown how objections are not the obstacles you might think they are, especially if you take steps to prevent them.

You're now at the point where you need to make the decision to focus more on the little things you've been doing that kill your deals. They're right in front of you, and you're just missing them. Everything you do with your customer matters to him/her, and too many salespeople blame customers for not buying from them rather than looking in the mirror and making the little changes you need to be better.

You need to stop and break down every little thing that you do, especially in the first ten minutes of meeting a customer and be more critical of how you appear to him/her. How you walk, how you talk, your facial expressions and body language, talking more than listening, and on and on—that's where you're losing deals—you just don't realize it.

Have someone video you as you first walk up to a customer, and I'll bet you change three things today.

But please, don't do NOTHING.

You might be angry with me when I say that, based on my observations over the years, I have concluded that most salespeople tend to be quite lazy. In many (if not most) commission-based sales businesses, a variety of circumstances naturally allow for a great deal of downtime for salespeople. Whether it's seasonality, inclement weather, rising interest rates, higher grocery prices, or numerous other uncontrollable, external forces that affect a company's customer traffic or business, downtime is going to occur in a salesperson's day—ikely on most workdays.

The typical reaction I see during these downtime periods with salespeople is frustration, worry, boredom, whining, anger, and who knows what other emotions because when there is downtime, they aren't making any money.

So, the first thing that needs to change—and right now—is your perception of downtime. Downtime is not playtime; it's time to be productive and improve your skill set with customers. Having some downtime to catch your breath, recover from a bad customer experience, overcome frustrations from losing a sale, or other stresses you need to handle is a **GIFT**.

However, the single biggest reason it is a gift is that (unlike many other professions) it is a time when salespeople can stop, catch their breath, analyze, and take specific actions that can prevent lost sales from happening in the future. It's a good time to reflect on what mistakes you made with your last customer, process what or how you can do it differently the next time, and how you can improve yourself in a one-step-at-a-time manner. And unlike most other non-sales-related professions out there, you can use that time to identify changes or actions that can improve how you handle the next customer.

To start, you will need to have some perspective on all of the negative influences that can generally affect the attitudes of commission salespeople daily. Here are just a few that come with the job.

- Poor training, no training, or no retraining
- Awful sales management
- A lack of recognition
- Handling the daily grind of customer rejection (reviewed in Chapter 12)
- Being over-managed or under-managed
- Being undercut by other salespeople
- The inconsistency of income
- Unattainable stretch goals from management
- Strong competition
- Favoritism with others getting more leads from management.

Or it could just be the constant barrage of customers saying "*No*" or that they "want to go home and think about it," never to be seen again, or just being worn down by dealing with customers who hate salespeople to begin with.

Guess what? Welcome to sales! The things listed above are just EXCUSES as to why salespeople miss the opportunity for a sale! These things are all normal and a small price to pay for having the opportunity to control your income with your own performance, as compared to other jobs where the superior performer gets paid exactly the same as the employee who does nothing all day. The good news is that in sales, we have a saying: "You eat what you kill," meaning that the more you sell, the more money you will make.

Here's a tip for all those excuses listed above: CHECK THEM AT THE DOOR because the pluses of a commission sales opportunity far outweigh those minuses. Get over it! Frankly, if you're not willing to get over it, you might as well punch out today and go home and update your resume.

Yes, constant customer interactions can emotionally wear you down--no doubt. To prevent that, you will need to build in periodic short-term time off to get away from it all. Get some rest, refresh, and come back ready to roll. Just look at the calendar for next year and build that in even before the year starts. Think prevention and take control over your time and emotions by getting away from it all here and there.

I also understand that at times, sales can be difficult because you are an individual performing in a team environment. It's different than any other hourly or salary-type position because you work with people you directly compete against. However, the income you can make is UNLIMITED in that scenario.

For successful salespeople, it ALL starts with building comfort, rapport, and trust with your customers, as stated in Chapter 4, "Building a Foundation of Trust." For a more detailed explanation of how to do that, pick up my second book entitled *No Trust, No Sale* at any online bookseller. Once you have read that, take some time to listen to my "No Trust, No Sale" Podcast series on Spotify, where I drill down even more on tips and tricks to build trust.

Once trust is built, you will have a great starting point on which to help your customer feel comfortable buying from you. Why? Because buying is more emotional than logical. It's a FEELING rather than the logical procedural steps most salespeople think it is.

All this has to begin with your buy-in to take action. We all have different ways to motivate ourselves toward a high sense of urgency, but I have found that getting paid is a great one. When in commission sales, you can make **whatever you want** for income. It's up to you, and the only one that can get in your way is YOU.

You also really do need to have a sales heart. When I was ten years old, living in the country in upstate New York, a farmer just down the road let me have some wood so I could build a little farmstand in front of our house. He also gave me a bunch of small clay pots he had outside his barn and was going to throw away. One morning, I dug up all the geraniums my dad had planted around our house, put them all in pots, and sold every one of them from this little stand by the road for $1.00 each. I felt like I had accomplished something really big; that feeling of selling was a very cool thing to me--at least until my dad got home. I won't get into detail here, but the discipline wasn't fun.

After all that, I realized that I had a salesperson's heart, which, after many years as a corporate executive and business owner, led me to what turned out to be my passion: helping others by selling them something that really made them happy and making some money doing it.

However, after some years in sales, I completely realized that it's the *art of the sale, not the science* that makes it all work. It's not what you do; it's how you do it. I promise you that your customers also approach working with a salesperson in the same manner. They buy from people they like and trust.

Too many salespeople forget that selling is about PEOPLE. Everything in the book that you just read, as well as my previous two books, is more about what makes people tick than the act of selling. I do not profess to be a psychologist, but it's just about treating people like THEY want to be treated, as Tony Alessandra says in his book The Platinum Rule, one of the best books I have ever read (1996).

Some of the selling systems that are out there can work if they are implemented correctly because many are based on psychological science; however, they must be implemented with the customer as the priority, NOT GETTING THE SALE, which is how many salespeople approach it.

All that aside, there are simply too many qualified salespeople out there treading water. They have a good month, then two bad months, then a good month--a picture of inconsistency because they are not taking the time to immediately break down every specific detail of the interaction they had with the customers who just walked out the door whether they purchased something from them or not.

Salespeople must take a few minutes to totally replay every step that just took place with the previous customer--what you said, how he/she reacted, and vice versa to determine the exact place where trust was built or lost. It needs to be identified exactly where you had the customer or where you lost the customer, so you can repeat what worked and change or adjust what didn't.

That kind of commitment to a detailed analysis is what is needed to hone your skills and craft the perfect message that will resonate with your customer—all built around the concept of trust.

In time, this detailed analysis, adjustment, and follow-through, using the concepts in this book as a cornerstone can help you avoid repeating the same mistakes and fine-tune what you do until you have it NAILED.

A Look in the Mirror Moment
In a look yourself in the mirror moment that can get the ball rolling

in the right direction, here are some hardcore questions to ask yourself right now.

- What's the first thing I do when a customer leaves without buying from me?
- What is the number one reason why customers haven't bought something from me in the last year?
- How can I improve my "meet & greet" with customers?
- How can I talk less and listen more in the first ten minutes of meeting a customer?
- What's the best way I can improve trust-building with customers?
- What will be my priority in downtime starting today?
- Going forward, how will I respond when my customer says, "I want to go home and think about it?"
- I need to **stop** doing this now: _____
- I need to **start** doing this now: _____
- I need to **continue** doing this: _____
- What's the number one developmental step I need to improve right now?

Answering these questions will get your mind in the self-improvement mode you need to be in to start taking your own independent action to improve your own skills, not waiting for a sales manager or trainer to do it. This is not about luck, karma, or magic. Your first step is to decide to be your own honest evaluator and then act on how to stop letting potential sales walk out the door with lame, phony excuses as to why they're not buying from you.

This is a Call to Action.

This is an opportunity to kick yourself in the backside and get going-- right now. It will take motivation and patience, but you can be who you set out to be if you do the work. Imagine where you can be if you commit daily to building trust with your customers, while sharpening your skills to help them buy from you. The opportunity is right in front of you, and so are the results!

DON'T LET ANYONE OR ANYTHING STAND IN YOUR WAY OF ACHIEVING THE RESULTS YOU SET OUT TO ACHIEVE!

LET'S BEGIN *SELLING FROM TRUST*!

Appendix

(The following are forms you can copy and use if desired.)

Responses to Typical Situations

Listed below are some typical situations every salesperson may face with a customer. For each one, write **what you currently say** to respond to that statement or situation. Also listed are a few alternative responses to consider, and after doing so, write how you plan to respond to each respective customer statement in the future.

1. "I'm/We're just looking"

My current response is _____
_____
_____
_____

Other possible responses are

"Well, you're in the right place to look. Let's talk about what would be perfect for you to look at, so I don't waste your time showing you the wrong thing."

"Great! What is it that you're here to see today?"

"I understand that you're shopping around.... We have a great selection to choose from. Let's talk about exactly what you're interested in, so I can show you right where that is."

"Great! Did you know that we're having a huge sale today?"

"Great! Well, that's where it starts, right? Where do we go from here?"
"I'm happy to assist you today.... Where would you like to get started?"

"Let's chat for a few minutes and find out exactly what would be perfect for you to look at today, sound good?"

"Great! Let's take a minute to make sure I have all the information I need to give you great service today, ok?"

"Ok great! Let's not worry about buying right now.... Just give me a little more information, and we'll go have some fun."

My new response is _____
_____
_____
_____

2. "This is the first place we've stopped"

My current response is _____
_____
_____
_____

Other possible responses are

"Have you looked at our website? Did anything catch your eye?"

"I'm happy that you've chosen us.... Many others have, as well, and I'm sure you'll be happy *that you did.*"

"I appreciate the opportunity to show you what we have.... I'm sure that you won't be disappointed."

"That's great! Most people make us the last stop because they are very happy with how we treat them here."

"So, after shopping online, what was the deciding factor in stopping here?"

"That's great! You're a guest here, so let me show you around. Would you like a coffee, water, etc.?"

"Our marketing department tells us that most customers have looked online before stopping in. Did you find anything on our website that caught your eye?"

My new response is _____
_____
_____
_____

3. "I have no idea what I want. I just started looking"

My current response is _____
_____
_____
_____

Other possible responses are

"That's fine…. Let's spend a few minutes together and find out what's the best fit for your needs."

"Here is a great place to start…. Let's sit for just a minute to get some more information, and we'll get started."

"I understand…deciding is a process, but I can help. Let's get started!"

"Great—you don't have to decide right now. Let's talk about what's important to you, and I'll take you right to that product."
"That's fine—did you have something specific in mind?"

"We have different models in stock. Let's talk for a minute, so I can eliminate what isn't a good fit for you. Sound good?"

"Great! Have you done any research online that can help us get started?"

My new response is _____
_____
_____
_____

4. The customer won't give you a budget

My current response is _____
_____
_____
_____

Other possible responses are

"We've got ____ of those here…did you want to start with the lowest priced model first or the highest priced?"

"Well, I can help you figure that out as we go.… What price range did you want to get started in today?"

"If you're like most of my customers, you have a rough idea of where you want to be in price. Since I want to be respectful of your budget, where did you want me to get started today?"

"We have ____ of those in the showroom, so what price range did you want me to focus on today?"

"I'm sure you both have the same goal…to find something you like in your price range, so where did you want to start today?"

"Since I will be very respectful of your budget, what is an amount that you don't want to exceed today?"

"If we started in a price range of $150/month, does that work for you?"

My new response is _____
_____
_____
_____

5. "I've/We've only got 10 minutes."

My current response is _____
_____
_____
_____

Other possible responses

"So when you say 10 minutes, does that mean you actually have to leave in 10 minutes?"

"That's not much time. What would be your expectations during those 10 minutes?"

"So, what you're saying is I only have about 10 minutes to impress you; is that right?"

"OK, sounds good…. What would be your goal for those 10 minutes?"

"That should be just enough time to talk and help me know what to show you when you come back in. Sound good?"

"Ok, so does that mean you know exactly what you want, and I should get the paperwork ready?"

(Smiling) "Now really…you only have 10 minutes?"

"That works…5 minutes for me to show you the perfect ____ , and 5 minutes for you to pay for it. Sound good?"

"That's not something that you can realistically do in 10 minutes. Do you want to make an appointment to come back?"

My new response is _____
_____
_____
_____

6. "I know what I want. I found it online, and I just want your best price for it."

My current response is _____
_____
_____
_____

Other possible responses

"So, if I give you our best price, you're willing to buy it right now?"

"I know price is important to you, but let's take a minute to make sure that it's the right product for you. Ok?"

"So, price is important to you. Is that what's most important to you in this purchase?"

"Sure, but how about we take a quick look at it to make sure it's the right fit for you?"

"Great that you found something that you like. If I can get some quick information from you, I might be able to find you something better for less money. Sound good?"

"Great…what did you like best about _____?"

"OK, great! What was it that you liked best about that _____?"

My new response is _____
_____
_____
_____

7. "I don't need a salesperson; I just want to go out and look at what you have."

My current response is _____
_____
_____
_____

Other possible responses are

"We like to work with our customers because our goal is to find the perfect _____ for you that's in your budget. How's that sound?"

"I'm sure your time is important to you…we have _____ of those in our showroom and lot. How about if we figure out exactly what you need, and I'll take you right to that?"

"It's important to me that you don't waste your time looking at something that's over your budget…. Let's talk for a minute, and I'll save you some time."

"I don't like working with a salesperson either, but I will be a trusted partner for you to help find something nice in your budget. Sound good?"

"You can certainly go out and look at what we have, but I know which product the sales manager is willing to make a deal on. So, is it ok if I go with you?"

"You can certainly go out and look, but some features that you don't necessarily need could inflate the price."

My new response is _____
_____
_____
_____

8. "The price is too high."

My current response is _____
_____
_____
_____

Other possible responses

"Our price is too high? What makes you think that?"

"I see that you have spent quite a bit of time researching the pricing at our competition. Have you also researched the company's integrity, service reputation, and commitment to customers?"

"I understand…. I wouldn't expect you to buy if we were way off on the price. So, let's talk about the price we would need to be at to earn your business today."

"We know that we are in the ballpark with our competition on pricing, but we would suggest that you look closely at how we stack up in service reputation and our warranty."

"Gosh, that's a little surprising to hear because we rarely miss a proposal by much, so let's give management an offer, at least one they could consider. Sound good?"

My new response is _____
_____
_____
_____

And then there's the one that we hear more than any other. If you hear this one, "as long as it's the right product that meets their needs or solves their problem," it is highly likely that the missing link at this point is a lack of trust with the salesperson that was not built earlier in the customer visit. Often, if asked, the customer won't be able to reveal exactly what it is that he/she is uncomfortable about but most often realize later on that it was a lack of trust.

9. "I want to go home and think about it."

My current response is _____
_____
_____
_____

Other possible responses

"I can appreciate that you want to go home and think about it because it's an important decision for you, but I would like to ask what it is that you would like to go home and think about?"

"Other than price, what else are you considering as part of your decision-making process?"

"It's been my experience that when customers say that they want to go home and think about it, it's either because they're out of time or are really not interested. Which one might it be for you?"

"You would like to think it over…. Would you care to expand on that, please?"

"Ok, fine. What did you plan on thinking about? Product? Price? Something else?"

"If you were me, what would you say to convince me to buy this today?"

My new response is _____
_____
_____
_____

There could be many more possible scenarios you need to be prepared for to have a quick and natural response. The *key* here is to identify every scenario that you may face with a customer and build a bank of responses that you are comfortable with after some practice. Over time, these responses or others that you develop will be at your disposal, and you will be able to field questions or challenges at a moment's notice.

Responses to Typical Situations (Blank Sheet)

Situation: _____

My current response is _____
_____
_____
_____
_____

Other possible responses are _____
_____
_____
_____
_____

My new response is _____
_____
_____
_____
_____

Name: _____

FOLLOW UP FOR TODAY
_____   ___/___/___

TO-DO

_____
_____
_____
_____
_____
_____
_____
_____

CALLS & EMAILS

_____
_____
_____
_____
_____
_____
_____
_____

APPOINTMENTS TODAY

_____
_____
_____
_____
_____

INTERNET RESEARCH

_____
_____
_____
_____
_____

Name: _____
FOLLOW UP FOR TODAY
_____   ___/___/___

TO-DO

_____

_____

_____

_____

_____

_____

_____

_____

CALLS & EMAILS

_____

_____

_____

_____

_____

_____

_____

_____

APPOINTMENTS TODAY

_____

_____

_____

_____

_____

_____

INTERNET RESEARCH

_____

_____

_____

_____

_____

_____

Name: _____

FOLLOW UP FOR TODAY

_____   ___/___/___

TO-DO	CALLS & EMAILS
_____	_____
_____	_____
_____	_____
_____	_____
_____	_____
_____	_____
_____	_____

APPOINTMENTS TODAY	INTERNET RESEARCH
_____	_____
_____	_____
_____	_____
_____	_____
_____	_____

SELLING FROM TRUST

Name: _____
FOLLOW UP FOR TODAY
_____   __/__/__

TO-DO	CALLS & EMAILS
_____	_____
_____	_____
_____	_____
_____	_____
_____	_____
_____	_____

APPOINTMENTS TODAY	INTERNET RESEARCH
_____	_____
_____	_____
_____	_____
_____	_____
_____	_____
_____	_____

Name: _____

FOLLOW UP FOR TODAY
_____ ___/___/___

TO-DO

_____

_____

_____

_____

_____

_____

_____

_____

CALLS & EMAILS

_____

_____

_____

_____

_____

_____

_____

_____

APPOINTMENTS TODAY

_____

_____

_____

_____

_____

_____

INTERNET RESEARCH

_____

_____

_____

_____

_____

_____

SELLING FROM TRUST

Name: _____
FOLLOW UP FOR TODAY
_____   ___/___/___

TO-DO

_____

_____

_____

_____

_____

_____

_____

_____

CALLS & EMAILS

_____

_____

_____

_____

_____

_____

_____

_____

APPOINTMENTS TODAY

_____

_____

_____

_____

_____

INTERNET RESEARCH

_____

_____

_____

_____

_____

Name: _____

FOLLOW UP FOR TODAY

_____   ___/___/___

TO-DO

_____
_____
_____
_____
_____
_____
_____
_____

CALLS & EMAILS

_____
_____
_____
_____
_____
_____
_____
_____

APPOINTMENTS TODAY

_____
_____
_____
_____
_____

INTERNET RESEARCH

_____
_____
_____
_____
_____

Works Cited

Allessandra, Tony. The Platinum Rule. Warner Books: New York. 1996.

ANAmarketers. "84 Percent of Purchases Come from Consumers Already Primed to Buy (Video)." YouTube. Jul. 2012

Cardone, Grant. LinkedIn. grantcardone.com/10xsummit. Nov. 2024.

Dale Carnegie. www.dalecarnegie.com. Oct. 2021.

"Nielsen Global Trust in Advertising Report." www.nielsen.com. Nov. 2025.

Tracy, Brian. Sales Pitch Mastery Speech. www.briantracy.com. Jan. 2023.

Tracy, Brian. "The Secret to Sales Success: Relationship Selling (Video)." YouTube. 13 Dec. 2024. https://www.youtube.com/shorts/iOPj99KJrZg.

Williams, Brian. "Sales Training: 21 Mind-Blowing Sales Stats." The Brevet Group. www.blog.thebrevetgroup.com/21mindblowingsalesstats. May 2013.

Acknowledgements

When I decided to write books about leveraging my success as a salesperson, sales manager, trainer, and coach to help others grow their businesses and increase their earnings, I wanted to create a step-by-step process that was realistic, sustainable, and based on the actual events and steps I personally used to achieve those same results.

My first book, *Know Your Customer*, was designed to raise awareness of who the buyer standing in front of you was, what made up his/her day before coming into your business, and how that might affect his/her approach, attitude, and, for some, the level of anxiety and how that might affect his/her ability to purchase something from you. My experience from dealing with hundreds of customers has taught me just how anxious they really are when working with most salespeople.

My second book, *No Trust, No Sale*, was intended to help salespeople understand the critical necessity of building trust in the early stages of a customer-interaction and how that can and will affect a customer's ability to buy no matter how good the price is or how perfect the product is. There are countless situations where salespeople can do everything right in following their selling system, delivering a great product presentation, and closing with sharpness and skill but still don't get the sale because they haven't built trust with those customers.

In *Selling from Trust*, I'm looking to build on the trust-building concepts from my first two books to understand who your customer is, how he/she prefers to work with a salesperson, and then complete the process by delivering the final and most important objective: to get him/her to say "Yes" to finally buying from you.

Acknowledgements

My first two books have been directly focused on the commission salesperson. However, when my last book, *No Trust, No Sale*, became available, I started to get feedback from people who purchased it from outside of that category. It made me sit down and think more deeply about why that happened and who my clients were. Of course, real estate agents, car salespersons, RV salespersons, cell phone salespersons, and furniture stores salespeople bought my book. However, finance managers, investment advisors, and general managers at golf courses stepped up and gave me feedback. I was thrilled to get compliments, feedback, and follow-up questions from pastors, doctors, chiropractors, dentists, roofing contractors, dental hygienists, health coaches, and others who I might not have previously considered book customers and/or coaching clients. After all, they deal directly with customers every day.

When you think about it, *anyone* who deals with the public in any format is in sales, even if he/she isn't specifically in a **commission** sales business, whether he/she realizes it or not. It brought to mind the fact that the key part of that process was that the salesperson isn't just selling a product or service, he/she is also selling himself/herself and building credibility as a trusted advisor, whom customers can rely on for advice and recommendations for the product or service he/she is trying to convince customers to purchase.

To build on that, I've asked a few of my book customers/businesspeople who are using those approaches and techniques to increase performance by building comfort, rapport, and trust with their customers and turning that into sales and success in their areas of expertise.

For my third book, *Selling from Trust*, I decided to interview some of those professionals and include their observations in this book because their comments, insights, and feedback contributed to the points I am trying to emphasize with my clients and customers. They provided solid contributions and feedback that helped me emphasize important suggestions that can help salespeople be more effective.

Acknowledgements

With that in mind, I would like to take this time to acknowledge the following business leaders, contributors, and feedback team for allowing me to interview them and share their personal experiences, as well as tips in many of the chapters in this book. They were also a valuable sounding board for me to bounce things off and offer comments and suggestions. Their words greatly contribute to helping support key points and adding value with their keys to success.

Many thanks to the following dedicated professionals who spoke at length with me to add valuable insight and keys to success that can help all our readers:

Ryan Meca, Vice President/Financial Advisor at Merrill Lynch,

Diane Luksis, Metabolic Health Coach,

Adam Isabella, Insurance Broker at The Morais Agency,

Erik Betz, long time Training & Development Specialist @ Alpin Haus,

Bob Rose III, CEO and Founder of Warrior Performance Group LLC

Brian Osborn, Real Estate Agent at Oasis Realty Collective

In addition to thanking the great contributors above, I would also like to acknowledge and recognize the following people on my BOOK LAUNCH TEAM, whose support and commitment to my latest book will be forever appreciated:

Joan Allen, Greg Clark, Bill Shufelt, Pastor Gary Clouse, Charles Weitz, Dr. Brandon Morris, Mark Hendershot, Brad Buyce, Dr. Jamie Chesler, Kirk Horan, Dayton King, Susan Giovanni Rick Munusami, Janet Metzger, Jill Leiberman, Kristen Stroebel, Jon Stroebel, Julie Foster, Tyler Daigler, Jared Falkowitz, and Jimmy Orapello.

Finally, I would like to thank my wife, Debbie, for her time and effort in proofreading and editing, as well as her honest advice, which served as my main sounding board for much of what you're about to read in this book, as with all the books I have published.

Thank you to all for your important contributions!

Acknowledgements

About the Author

Thomas Morin enjoyed a highly successful twenty-five-year executive-level career with a large retail grocery chain in upstate New York, continuously getting promoted through the system as a store manager, human resource specialist, district manager, zone director, and director of the store labor and expense department, managing over $300 million in labor costs for one hundred retail stores. During his career, Thomas managed over 16,000 employees, directing them to deliver superior customer service and salesmanship that maximized every opportunity to achieve excellent sales performance.

His career progressed to business ownership in the golf industry for several years, after which he joined Alpin Haus in Amsterdam, New York, a nationally recognized top fifty RV sales company. There, he distinguished himself as a leading salesperson and discovered his passion for mentoring and training sales professionals. He was quickly promoted to sales manager, leading his team to consecutive record-setting sales years. He was promoted to director of employee development, where he trained, coached, and developed all the salespeople in the company.

During that tenure, Thomas developed a company sales playbook, used as a key sales training tool for the company, as well as the cornerstone for all new salesperson training.

Eventually, Thomas retired from corporate life and relocated to North Myrtle Beach, South Carolina, where he expanded his sales playbook, which became the starting point as a certified life and sales coach, advising, training, and coaching salespeople in all business ventures from all across the United States. To help communicate and expand his proven trust-building, selling from the bottom-up method, Thomas became a sales author, starting with his book *Know Your Customer*, where he wrote about emphasizing the key information salespeople must learn about their customers to provide the best possible customer service and salesmanship.

Thomas followed that up with his highly successful book *No Trust, No Sale*, which focused on the key elements of trust-building that salespeople must establish for customers to feel comfortable buying from them. In his follow-up book, Thomas also emphasized identifying each customer's individual type and then adjusting communications and product demonstrations to a way that the customer would be most receptive to, as customers prefer to buy from someone they like and trust

As a follow-up, Thomas created the "No Trust, No Sale" podcast series on Spotify, iTunes, and Amazon with ten podcasts that took a deeper dive into how (and why) to build trust with customers to increase opportunities for happier customers and better sales results.

In this latest book, *Selling from Trust*, Thomas identifies the steps that salespeople need to follow, now that trust has been built to bring the sale to the finish line and have the customer say "Yes" to buying. He also addresses how customers have changed and the common obstacles that salespeople typically face (and must overcome) to build the consistency needed to sustain long-term success.

About the Author

Each of Thomas's books complements his knowledge and expertise in training and coaching salespeople to achieve desired sales results and solid income in a challenging industry and to establish and maintain a successful sales career that stands the test of time.

Thomas has emerged as a successful trainer and mentor, coaching salespeople one-on- one on how to adapt their approach with customers in "meet & greet," rapport-building, and individual selling style to a way that best fits the style of the customer with whom they are currently working. He is also in his third year as a feature column writer for RV Pro Magazine, a monthly and nationwide RV industry publication.

For more information about Thomas, his books, podcasts, and coaching opportunities, check out his website at www.unlockyoursalescareercoaching.com.

If you need to reach out with questions or comments to Thomas, you are welcome to do so by emailing him at bookauthorcoach@gmail.com.

Thomas Morin is the President of Unlock Your Sales Career Coaching LLC, providing one-on-one consultation and coaching to commission salespeople across the country to help build stronger customer relationships that increase confidence in purchasing.

Thomas's coaching program also collaborates with clients to assess strengths, weaknesses, and career goals, and helps increase average gross deals and commissions, whether clients are new to commission-based sales or are seasoned professionals.

Thomas is respectful of company-sponsored sales systems and looks to expand sales skills by focusing on areas typically not included, such as handling customer anxiety, reading body language, and identifying (and adjusting to) customers' type. This builds customer comfort, rapport, and trust, while reducing tension in decision-making.

There are a variety of coaching packages to best fit each client's specific needs and situation. Thomas's website is www.unlockyoursalescareercoaching.com. He can be contacted for further information as follows.

Email: bookauthorcoach@gmail.com
Phone: 518-428-2429
Website: Click on the **contact now** link at the bottom of his website

Morin's Previous Books

www.ingramcontent.com/pod-product-compliance
Ingram Content Group UK Ltd.
Pitfield, Milton Keynes, MK11 3LW, UK
UKHW022239230426
12048UKWH00018BA/1347